RUTHLESS CAMPAIGN

A Woman's Guide to Political Victory

J D HERMAN

outskirtspress

DENVER, COLORADO

For

Martin Herman
The Treasure of the Sierra Nevada

Contents

Introduction

THE FIRE IN your belly bemoans all reason. You want to make a run for a local down ticket elected office. What will bomb blast your soul and shake your will, is that within 48 hours of filing for office your past will be like a county fair pretzel, twisted into salty tasty stories meant to humiliate, disgrace and shame you into surrendering.

Politics is a blood sport. It is a world of lies, malice, rudeness and great expectations. Some of you *will* get bruised, tattered and crushed by the political machine, but with a good memory and a professional, responsible and ruthless campaign...*wait a time with patience* and get your revenge later.

After you win, Titans do whatever it takes to get control; they want to own you. Then again, you might lose, and if that happens—you will matter to no one. You will resemble the weight of a newborn child: people always ask, but no one cares.

Win or lose, most people will be in awe; you are the ballsy chick that had the guts to run for public office, stayed the course, threw some punches, followed some fashion rules, learned to speak in public, counted her votes and pandered to the multitudes.

PART ONE

GET READY!

★ ★ ★

"I'm going to fight hard. I'm going to give them hell."

Harry S. Truman 17 September 1948

Why Are You Running for Office?

THERE YOU ARE at the Operating Engineers annual picnic, breaking a vow to never eat anything with a face, and then, after relishing a plateful of chicken wings and a beer you are oh so slow, to wipe BBQ sauce off those greasy fingertips.

To top off the egregious offense to vegetarian principles, off you go traipsing around, finding a cozy corner to chat with so-called political soul mates. You rationalize that it's just an innocent mingle with the Titans of the community; to whom you pretend to savor every sentence they utter.

Finally, after being seen eating animal fat and swooning over Titans (Titans are the movers and shakers, contributors, gate-keepers, stakeholders and/or community leaders), you act a little indignant when a friend says, *"Good grief, you're acting just like a Politician."*

While you may be awash in disgrace, stay calm. What you need to devise is a private reason, a personal motto, jingle or a mantra that will calm any trepidations of the label: Pol (aka-politician). This rationale or personal motivation is a secret inspiration: probably based on ego or deceit. It's not a public campaign slogan, it is a secret.

Being a Pol is a journey based on good decisions and secrets. Pols must keep secrets and this is a biggie. Outwardly, you confidently smile and inwardly a primordial mantra will be darting across your right brain. Tuck this top-secret mother of all rationalizations safely into your subconscious, with the aim to keep the fire in the belly stoked

---

PRIVATE RATIONALES FOR SEEKING OFFICE

★ I need a job
★ I want to expose the corruption
★ I need money and power

---

and the Energizer Bunny spirit drumming even when the polls show you down by ten points two weeks out from the primary.

Self-Assessment

NOW LET'S EVALUATE strengths and weaknesses through self-assessment and self-discovery; so the secret rationale will not be obvious and some poor life choices won't be outed or spun into negatives that can be exploited by the opposition.

Self assessment is to prepare you for the best and worst case scenario. The worst is when opponents dig up dirt you never thought anyone would find out or even guess: and the best, when an opponent uncovers a little known negative and you are prepared with a plausible albeit brief explanation of what, when and why.

When your negatives are exposed, there will be political mayhem. Count on mayhem during the campaign. That means, be prepared for the eventuality of the rebellious bits and pieces of your life to leak out. Both constituents and campaign contributors will judge you on your ability to ward off assaults. The excuses and explanations you concoct do matter.

Let's be brutally honest, drop out now if you are queasy about tainting or destroying the people you cherish. Ask the following questions; if the answer is yes to even one of these questions then I trust you will not run for office—until there is a family resolution.

Are there more than two things about my personal and/ or business life that I am loath for anyone to know? Will my muddy little secrets expose dirtier family secrets? Is it worth it to watch my family writhe in social anguish when a secret is unexpectedly exposed? Will people I treasure be irreparably hurt when some or all of our family's secrets are exposed?

All right then, not a single "Yes."

Now, let's take a look at all those padded résumés you have sent out the past ten years. The facts may not line up. Don't you dare find yourself using three years with a fortune 500 company as a basis for a qualification; and then hear an opponent tell an audience, *"She worked two years and a month, not three years and they gave her a pink slip."* Accuracy is essential on the candidate résumé and while reviewing your life history.

Create some sort of personal timeline. Connect three or four pieces of yellow legal paper together with glue or tape: mark a line down the middle. Note on the line in chronological order everything relevant about your life and the people closest to you. Everyone counts: siblings, parents, cousins, in-laws are all part of your research. Bottom-line everyone in your family: both their achievements and atrocities are fair game and fodder to the opponent's research teams—that's why ferreting out the truths about your personal history is imperative.

For a no holds barred investigation of you and your life check out ZabbaSearch.com, CampaignSecrets.com and/or NetDetective. com. Check your credit-worthiness through the three main agencies: Experian, Equifax and TransUnion. There are also ways to check Personal Information Reports about your employment and liens and judgments, Choice Point Full File Disclosure, Insurance Services Offices and Medical Information Bureau are all reliable sources too.

In addition, you must see how you rate on Teletrack and Central Credit—there are even more links to investigating yourself at Komando.com/news. Kim Komando's website is chockfull of timely information. Kim Komando hosts the nation's largest talk radio show about computers, writes a syndicated weekly column: Tech Time, and is all over the Internet. Komando warns us that personal information, found in public records may be incorrect. It is your responsibility to find and fix any erroneous information before the opposition gets a hold of it—and slaughters your momentum with lies or innuendo.

Do not worry about obvious skeletons in the family closet, later on, in Part 2—Get Set! I will share a few techniques for pivoting to plausible and verifiable explanations.

I know of two candidates who found themselves exposed to negative press after an alternative newspaper published stories about former husbands. One candidate's husband was doing hard time for driving under the influence (DUI), and the other husband had done time for something related to medical malpractice. One of the candidates just ignored the negative press and the other had a plausible explanation. The voters ignored the negatives and both candidates eventually won public office.

That said: know if a third cousin is in the slammer and why, know the family credit history, driving records, and health and wellness issues. You can be sure the opposition is snooping around property tax records, driving by your house, maybe digging through your garbage cans, talking to neighbors and friending you with a fake name on Facebook.

Negative opposition research and political campaigning go hand in hand. It is one of our political system's ways of winning at all costs. Negative campaigning is how the political business works. Do not for one minute think your opponents are not going to hunt down your negatives and distort any positives to their advantage.

An assault from an opponent by whisperers, told to a journalist, appearing in the local paper front page, above the fold, on the Friday morning before the Tuesday election would lose you the election. It is better to change your mind and not run instead being bludgeoned or whacked up the side of the head—by an event you thought was hidden or long forgotten.

The grimy painful self-inflicted process of examining your life and your family's life is tantamount to dumping dirty laundry on the kitchen table. Fact checking your life is not an option—it is an imperative to know the strengths and weaknesses of your work and social history and your financial and spiritual history.

Spirituality use to be a private matter. We all pretty much assumed political ethics and integrity were akin to a spiritual essence. At least, that's what most of us use to believe. I hope you believe a spiritual essence coupled with integrity and ethics is an important visible ruthless candidate trait.

But, before I tackle the grimy side of who you have to be, there are still a few more personal questions and assessments to take in consideration. Later, in Part 1—Get Ready! I will describe a few temptations and how to shave off some integrity when you run with the wolves.

While you are wondering if you should seek office, here are some stimulating questions to mull over, remember, it is not *if* the opposition finds out rather it is *when* the opposition finds out.

You must know yourself inside and out.

Work and Social History Q and A

★ What is your work experience?
★ Are there any work gaps.
★ If so what did you do?
★ What clubs do you belong?
★ What positions have you held within the clubs?
★ How many times have you been married?
★ What religion are you?
★ Do you believe in the Rapture?
★ Have you ever had a bankruptcy?
★ How many years ago? Why?
★ What was your income for the last three years?
★ What does your credit history look like?
★ What is your credit number?
★ Do you own or rent?
★ What is your payment history?
★ Do you pay property taxes on time?
★ Is your backyard attractive?
★ Is your home & front yard attractive?
★ What kind of car do you drive?
★ Is the car's exterior clean?
★ Any speeding tickets?
★ Drunk driving
★ Reckless driving convictions?
★ Are there drug users in the family?
★ Any calls for service from the police to your home in the last 10 years?
★ What is your military experience?
★ Do you smoke?
★ Do you drink at local bars?

Personal Inventory Q and A

★ Take a snapshot of yourself. Are you unkempt, poorly dressed or overweight?

★ Does the local newspaper have a flattering or unflattering snapshot of you?

★ Are your teeth straight and white? Are there any missing when you smile?

★ Does your Mother ever tell you to stand up straight? Can you?

★ What do your hands look like? How are your cuticles and nail polish?

★ Are you shoes sensible, scuffed, old fashioned or stylish?

★ Do you practice and have knowledge of both current and basic etiquette?

★ What happens to your voice in anger, humiliation, excitement and/ or fear?

★ Can you control your voice when it begins to squeak like a middle school boy?

★ Do you cough or clear your throat when nervous?

★ Do you know when to use a firm handshake or a weak shake?

★ Do you know when to double air kiss, hand grasp, arm pat and double back pat?

★ Is your hairdo age appropriate, and are the roots inconspicuous?

★ Do you work out? Is it obvious that you don't work out?

Some of the answers to these questions will come from your online investigations and some you'll need to ponder in front of a mirror. In addition to personal inventory, work and social history Q and A's, go further and start thinking about covertly taking friends and family down memory lane.

To avoid a self assessment as your sole historical fact check; telephone some old friends. First, make a list of your successes and the people that helped to get you where you are today. Reflect what friends and colleagues may say about you. this is tougher than you might think, because we all believe we have accomplished much more than the truth.

Next, hunt for the phone numbers of those mentors, guides and friends that helped you get to where you are now. Call all of them just to say hello and reminisce about the good times and successes you've had together. There is no need to tell them you are running for public office.

Of course, you appreciate why this phone call is an important part of self-assessment. Former colleagues might be forgetful— they may need a reminder of your friendship and past collective successes and you might too. Also, when friends or family are asked by the opposition or media about you, the "nostalgic corroboration" reminisce will be on the top of everyone's minds.

Temptation, Spirituality and Ethics are a Dilemma

MARK TWAIN UNDERSTOOD, "there are several good protections against temptation, but the surest is cowardice." Being a coward, fear of jail or humiliation will make you a better candidate.

I was a coward. I had a line in the sand, a sense of morality that could not be extinguished by temptation. I had ideals. Let us call these ideals, newbie political scruples. If you think you have ideal political scruples, well then my dear, you have not been beaten down or been offered enough. We all have our price. I did not find my upper limit, but I watched others find theirs. That is why I push to know yourself and the limits of your cowardice, just in case you get in over your head.

In life, just like in a campaign, being tested and retested on your baseline integrity and ethics is a given. Integrity, coupled with honesty, is simply doing the right thing for the right reasons. Ethics is a little different—it's like good grooming; it's always attractive, but not always a political virtue. Former President Clinton hinted that character and integrity mingle and may be hard to pin down when he told us, *"Character is a journey, not a destination."*

That same journey may be your path too. The ruthless candidate has a fundamental job of weaving integrity and ethics without looking like a whistleblower, a dirty rat or the anti-Christ. Voters want to believe that you are "The One"—the one politician who has unflinching ethics and integrity and the ability to get things done. Let the voters have their dreams: just don't get caught *not* being "The One." You are not a saint or the real "One"—Elvis took that spot years ago, what you are is a ruthless candidate that has good character.

As a candidate, don't overtly define your character, the voters define character, by what they see you doing and by what the opponent unearths in your background. I am not advocating a religious character either, however, it's gonna come up and soon. So, when a question about your religious character comes up in polite conversation, why not have already decided on a guide—not explicit, but fundamental to being ethical: so, how about the Ten Commandments? The nice thing about a few of those ten principles is, if you break some of them, it's possible to ask for forgiveness and go on your merry way. Just ask former Speaker, Senator Newt Gingrich.

Intertwined in the Ten Commandments, with a loose knot, are political ideals. I think you will agree: common sense and a principal of ethics simply mean no blasphemy, murder, theft or adultery. Although not explicit, there is also an obligation to truthfulness, honor of parents and not coveting others possessions. Your line in the sand, adhering to the Ten Commandments, is not solely from a religious perspective. Your line in the sand must come from the gut, from cowardice, from G-d, and from how lucky you feel.

I would not blab all over town how your political or religious ideals surpass the incumbents' or opponents'. Keep in mind, a run for office is not an appointment to West Point Military Academy, along with a sworn code of honor to *"...not lie, cheat or steal, nor tolerate those who do."* The current crop of elected Pols (Pols is short for politicians) probably won't be happy to hear about your honesty, integrity or ethics—so be careful what and how it is said. Pols know what they have become and are often chagrin about what they have done to get and keep power. Most could not pass an integrity lie detector test.

Pols emanate confidence, but that glow may be devilish and not from pride. On the outside, aloof and self-assured, while inside there is a palatable glow of self-loathing. Most of the Pols I know, when prodded about their political life are pompous and not the least apologetic for their sins.

Why, a few years ago, a crowd was mystified and a bit horrified when a long time local state senator, now deceased, told a crowd, *"Don't tell my mother I'm a politician. She thinks I'm a piano player in a whorehouse."* Just last week, I heard a former Nevada Congresswoman admitted, *"Within six months of being elected I was running with the herd. You have to."*

The ruthless candidate understands she will have to run with the herd. Religious fervor is just one leg of the race. In the United States being private about religious zeal or exhibiting a complete *lack* of it, is not smart. Preening religiosity by sporting a cross when visiting church groups will not kill you. However, a Jet's football star Tebowing prayer stance is overdoing it. Adhering loosely to religiosity is a fundamental obligation and tactic of the ruthless candidate.

Somewhere within the 9/11 timeline, religion became the undeterred beast of politics. True, there are secular people in your town. However, most seculars believe they are a Christian of some sort and they will like to think you too are a closet Christian. Seculars and Christians alike will give more value to what you say; if they believe there are shared common values.

A recent political communication research web site, www. presidentalrhetoric.com, has a review of David Domke and Kevin Coes' treatise, *The God Strategy: How Religion became a Political Weapon*. They say if a Pol truly wants to succeed and excel in today's political environment she *must* embrace not only religiosity—but use spiritual talk.

> *What has developed ...is a no-holds-barred religious politics that seeks to attract voters, identify and attack enemies, and solidify power... sometimes these signals are intended for the eyes and ears of all Americans, and other times they are distinctly targeted to specific segments of the population.*

It is important to hang on to some covert code words to prove you are on familiar ground with Christian Evangelicals and New Age thinkers. The easiest value laden Christian dialogue to prove and show your spiritual worth to any doubting Thomas is to mention the Ten Commandments. In addition, to understand the non-secular voters' thinking, study two recent films; both of which are on DVD.

First, download the documentary, *The Secret,* a 2006 film produced by Prime Time Productions. *The Secret* is a series of interviews that emphasizes the idea of expecting or believing everything one wants or needs, one will receive. The trick, the film emphasizes, is that you should be constantly thinking about what you want and to maintain a positive emotional state while you are thinking about getting whatever it is you want. The antithesis to garbage in—garbage out: except G-d is in charge, not you.

The other Christian film is the drama, *Fireproof.* It's a 2008 Samuel Goldwyn Film, directed by Alex Kendrick, who co-wrote and co-produced it with Stephen Kendrick. The storyline describes a rocky marriage and how, the husband Caleb, goes on a 40-day dare. It is worth a watch to understand the leap of faith some Evangelicals believe they have taken to be born again.

Jezebel may have been the first mean girl. Revelations 2:20

Taking a jump from being religious to being a political party disciple is a real leap of faith. Nonetheless, the similarities of a political party devotee and stalwart religiosity are comparable. Your party affiliation, religion and depth of conviction (or lack of either) is a potential problem. When a candidate is filled with political party dogma and religiosity, it is reasonable you might stray from one or the other.

A personal conflict between political and religious dogmas is precarious. Being all one or all the other will unbalance the campaign. You are bound to lose votes. Each dogma has adamant and abundant beliefs, in two very different systems and styles of governing. When the ruthless candidate tries to be all things to all people it confuses the moderate, causes rifts within the righteous, splits the vote of the Independent and confounds the party loyal voter. To confuse any voter in any way is to ask for trouble.

OK, so consider you may be an ideologist, and if so; the question has to be how committed are you to the party line and platform or a religious dogma? Conflicting convictions is an impediment for a down ticket ruthless candidate. you probably must be one or the other: Conservative Republican Religious Nut or Progressive Liberal Democrat Fanatic.

Fanatic, Hack, Christian, Evangelical, Conservative, Progressive, Constitutionalist, Libertarian or OccupyYucaipa: it's sensible to pick a side and hang with those like-minded people: namely the officials, voters and Titans who are on your side of your the ideological fence.

Pick a side and stick to that side; candidates know better than to be a flip-flopper, but flip-flopping is what it is called every time you change an ideological direction. That's why you should be really careful when you change your mind about anything.

Not to be too redundant but, flip-flopping, about religious or political beliefs, is not against the law; however, you still should never change your mind, even if the facts don't line up. Titans (community leaders and often-big campaign donors), religious zealots and party line voters get confused and eventually disenchanted with a flip-flopping candidate. Ethically speaking, everyone should change their minds when the facts don't jibe.

Flip-Flopping is a mistake and you are going to make mistakes, that's' why being skillful with public excuses is imperative to the newbie candidate. Before you create a public excuse for a flip-flop or a negative; do what every Pol must do: decide if the negative is a character flaw (can't be fixed—drop out now) or an incident. Write and practice giving an excuse, by using a **justification, explanation, defense** or an **apology.**

A justification is a vindication or an attempt to prove what you did was just and you believe the voter will exonerate you.

> If you leave here with just one idea about me leaving my district…..please keep in mind the urgency of a lung cancer diagnosis and chemotherapy.
>
> My husband of two months came to me with an x-ray that showed two cancerous growths, in his left lung. Ninety-five percent of people with this diagnosis die soon.
>
> It never occurred to me not to stay by his side. Marty is sitting here in the audience. I call him the Treasure of the Sierra Madre.

The explanation is to create the short truth about how you acted in a clear and intelligent manner.

> Regardless of what you have heard before….here is what happened. I saved my husband's life. I rented my house to the head of a Christian homeless Vet organization and rented a one room apartment in my district.
>
> I received my mail, washed and ironed my clothes and prepared meals and kept my personal computer and telephone at my apartment.
>
> During the day I attended to my duties as a Councilwoman and my brave, bald, and very thin husband went to work too.
>
> At night I slept at my husband's home; trying to fix nourishing food that he could tolerate and helping him to keep positive after the five chemotherapies.

The defense is a statement of what you had to do as a protective act or as a plea to understand the circumstances and to remind your audience of your virtue.

> Even if you disagree with my decision to sleep outside of my district for four months, here are the facts: As soon as I learned that my husband of two months had lung cancer, I rented my house to the head of a Christian homeless Veterans organization and rented a one room apartment in my district.
>
> I left my furniture in the garage at my house; I kept my clothes at my apartment, but yes... I did sleep outside my district for over four months.
>
> Who in this room would not do the same thing for their husband, wife or family member?

Or the apology is asking for a vindication or asking to be excused for the issue that happened in the past and resulted with you paying a price.

> It never occurred to me that staying at my husband's home while he recuperated from surgery and chemotherapy was wrong. I knew the law and sincerely believed that I displayed a sincere intent of living and serving in my district.
>
> We were working with a realtor from my district and Marty put his home on the market.
>
> I left my furniture in the garage at my house, I kept my clothes at my apartment, but yes, I did sleep outside my district for over four months.
>
> I regret not asking permission from the City Attorney before I made the decision to sleep outside my district. Because of that oversight, I am paying the price.

Begin the public excuse directly and without any arrogance. Use only one example because the audience seldom hears more than one, and that is also why I say limit the mea culpa to a five-sentence response. Avoid any jokes or humor. While giving an excuse, the compulsory body language and facial stance shows the audience, you are clear on the behavior or deed, but strong enough in your leadership qualities to deflect the negative.

Act kind, be serious without being beaten, look your accuser in the eye and do not argue or give a lame excuse. Try not to let your eyelids flicker like a schoolgirl caught in a lie. Stick to the topic and answer only the question posed. Be one tiny part indignant and two parts kumbaya, and never be perceived as haughty.

With practice deception is easy. A talented politician never ever says she is sorry and seldom acknowledges a mistake. However, if you make a thoughtless statement like, *"I don't care about the poor, they have a safety net...'* or ...*'I like to fire people..."* I suggest you man-up as former Governor Mitt Romney did and simply say: *"I misspoke."* The word misspoke, in Pol speak, is the same as, *"I made a mistake."*

The eyes will give you away. Never look away or cast your eyes downward. Use what I call a Pol's defensive soft Bambi-doe eye. It is a direct glance of sorrow, but not pleading. Master this look of sorrow. Your mouth, softly shut with corners of your lips up slightly, and the brow also lifted just slightly. Sometimes you may also tuck the chin into your neck ever so slightly.

Use care with the additional tucked-chin technique. When you tilt you head you might be misunderstood. Those around you will wonder if you are miming them. If the eyes are open too much, you will look like a Pol caught in the headlights, and if the lips are up too much in the corners you'll look like the "Joker" in Batman. To master the sincere soft Bambi-doe eye, brows up and tilted chin: use a mirror and take some time to practice.

Code of Ethics

For the down ticket candidate, codes of ethics are loosely written rules of decorum. While often not enforced, those rules are both a responsibility to acknowledge and useful tools to use against your opponents. That said, it is essential to know state statutes and never deviate from those statutes. Watch yourself and always stealthily police all your opponents, to make sure they are adhering to all the rules.

While most towns have reams of ignored written codes of ethics; unless a formal complaint is made—breaking those rules doesn't pose a problem. Even when the City Attorney takes the code of ethics seriously, it may take months for an ethics commission to hear and rule on a complaint. There are rarely ramifications if you do not follow the code of ethics. They are usually just for show.

Frankly, unless you have really ticked off the District Attorney or the City Attorney hates your guts, or one or both of them is a staunch supporter of the political group you don't belong to, there will be a reprimand but no jail time.

Not going to the slammer for breaking the local code of ethics is reassuring; that said, remember not to poke a stick at enemies. It is not ok to taunt or tempt fate. At the least, remember: never get caught not following those laws and statues. If you are caught breaking a <u>local</u> code of ethics, act a tiny bit indignant and surprised; then deny it and wait it out.

One rule to never break is to attend or participate in a closed door meeting. The first time you experience one, you may not even recognize the serious breach of public trust. Like the well-known saying, written by the former Supreme Court associate justice, Potter Stewart, *"...I don't know what porn is, but I know it when I see it."*

A closed-door meeting is nothing more than three or more

people gathering in an obscure venue. For our purposes, an illegal meeting is a closed-door meeting/ backroom meeting (aka smoke-filled room) where back room deals are discussed. You may not know you are in a closed-door/ back room meeting. At first, the purpose of the closed-door meeting is not obvious—but, just like porn... said Justice Stewart; you will know it when you see it. When you find yourself in a closed-door meeting, it will be a test of your integrity, ethical standards and candidate cunning.

You will receive an invitation to attend one of these meetings, so be prepared to be tested. Please, do not hurriedly gather your papers, grab your purse in a huff—while shrieking, *"this meeting is illegal!"* and as you rush out, trip on the rug. More to the point, ask yourself, does the need to be trusted, accepted and respected, by current elected officials and other opponents, win out over acting like a wide-eyed bunny and hightailing it to safety?

A closed-door meeting will cause integrity, ethics and political purpose to collide. Attending closed-door meetings and making decisions in those meetings may complicate life but usually all you have to say is "I am sorry" or "I will never attend one of those meetings again." If you are accused of attending a closed-door meeting: deny it and wait it out. If you are caught attending a closed-door meeting—admit your ignorance and pledge to never attend one again. Then, tout your ethics by writing a new code of ethics for the community. One guy, wrote a code of ethics guide—after he was caught red handed attending a back room meeting! And now I hear he has the nerve to run for a judgeship.

Here's a way to join the corrupt Pols and opponents in a closed-door meeting and leave before any illegal or unethical act has been committed. Listen to what I have to say. Don't blow this opportunity to pretend to be a real Pol.

Here is the exit plan: when you sense a secret closed-door meeting: simply glance down at your cell phone and say, *"Oh no,"* put your hand to your heart or cheek and in a quiet disappointed tone say, *"You'll have to excuse me."* Then smile weakly and make a slow but deliberate getaway. Do not give an excuse.

The problem with this avoidance and leave-taking is you won't know how the Titans, Pols, and opponent(s) may have arrived at a mutual agreement. So before you take leave, invite yourself to an alternative secret meeting, *"If I don't get back soon, where are you all going for drinks?"*

Worst case, you do not catch up with them later. If you don't, you will never know how they deliberated and came up with decisions. On the other hand, they want to know where you stand on the issue. That means they will smile and say, *"See you at the Prospectors Club around 6?"*

NOT TO BELABOR INTEGRITY and character, but they do matter. They matter because this is the perceived reputation of you. If you think you might deliberately help friends, family, Titans, other Pols—either overtly or clandestinely feed at the public trough, then the next section about integrity and ethics is just for you.

The act of deliberately helping friends feed at the public trough is not necessarily dishonest, but if the intent is to leave others out of the deliberations on, say, a non bid contract for your niece, a zoning change or a secret meeting with the Chamber of Commerce; then your nepotism or friendship gifts might indicate a lack of political and personal honesty. Getting caught or being accused of doing favors in political dealings is certainly not a clever political tactic.

My best advice is to try *not* to be caught or exposed. Well, technically, the best advice is not to do anything illegal or dishonest to begin with. Everyone does favors for others and a few get caught. Accepting and putting envelopes stuffed with cash in the freezer is passé. Accepting anything quid pro quo is asking for jail time. If you get caught: first, act just a tad indignant, deny it and wait it out.

Sometimes, if you have the right friends in high places, the problem mends itself.

That said, consider the gut warning. I know you have an inner gut voice, the warm adrenaline rush in the pit of the stomach, that feeling that makes you squirm a little and says: *"uh oh, this is not right."* So no blubbering on TV or to the editorial board, "I am so sorry to have let my family and constituents down." Attending smoke filled meetings in back rooms, taking money and doing favors for friends and family indicates you have fallen to a temptation, have some misplaced integrity or forgotten common-sense ethical standards.

Meanwhile, if you do favors—make them count—have a record of everyone you have ever helped through any political or social process. Showing integrity might get you elected but being ruthless is what makes a true politician. Establish your bona fides by keeping track of what you do, and for whom, and remind those people when it suits your needs.

In other words if you help anyone, by word or deed, during the campaign—record the favor. If there is a dalliance with a Titan (contributor, mover and shaker or a fellow Pol); keep it to yourself but record it somewhere—in code—on the page titled paybacks. Record in a bound booklet, everything that is asked of you by Titans, contributors and voters. Hide this little black book of good deeds in your lingerie drawer—or better yet a safety deposit box or a home safe. It is important for long-term political survival to make weekly updates of who, what, where and when a pal was helped out.

Primarily, the good deed book is most important when you campaign for reelection. Some may say that it's probably better not to write a quid pro quo down—but how will you remember all of the people that owe a favor?

So, is this form of political ruthlessness, the keeping track of what you do and for whom unethical? I don't think so, as long as you don't get caught and you are not overtly candid when asked why you made a decision. Don't ever openly refer to the little book of good deeds; ..."let me see, I wrote, on February 16, I had drinks with the Titans at the bowling stadium private bar...later the guy from a network called me for what I interpreted to be a booty call..."

I think it's time to make up your mind what kind of Pol will work for your personality. Let's face it; you aren't really sure what kind of a politician you'll be—yet. Will you feign religiosity? Or, be a coward (to stay in check). You don't know if you will attack like a junk yard dog or piddle on the ground when temptation raises its ugly head. That said, if you aren't clear about the limits of your integrity, then forgetaboutit for now and get back to the question of ethics later.

You might not be invited to closed-door meetings, let alone the Operating Engineers annual community picnic, after you explore neighborhood problems and solutions and decide which side of the fence you will ride. To not be included—that alone should be an incentive to know about every problem and solution for your community.

The Vision Speech

FORMER PRESIDENT GW Bush is said to have referred to his vision speech as, *"oh, yeah, the vision thing."* Obviously, he did not relish the idea of harping on the problems and solutions of the country in speech after speech. After awhile you too will get tired of saying the same vision speech repeatedly. However, the *vision thing* is the crux of the political game and you must be good at composing and delivering it.

This book's definition of a vision speech is the problems and solutions of neighborhoods and communities, given in the form of a casual answer when you are asked why you are running for office. The vision speech is given at a debate or public appearance when the Master of Ceremonies instructs you: "Candidate A (that's you) you have one minute to introduce yourself."

The issues in a vision speech are a combination of the issues you have ferreted out while talking to the voters and the Titans; and the solutions you strongly and unwaveringly support. The problems and solutions are your platform planks. Those planks are put in plain words within a vision speech.

A stump speech is a vision speech—only longer and more often recited at club meetings or large gatherings with multi issued constituents. Both a stump speech and a vision speech may contain ideology from your political party coupled with a vision for improvement of the community and some Christian cryptograms too.

BEFORE YOU OPEN YOUR MOUTH ABOUT ANY ISSUE, FOLLOW THE MONEY AND THE POWER. First, identify issues that you know Titans will expect you to advocate. It is understandable that you think this is ass backward. Wait, you are wondering—shouldn't I pick issues, and then find the people who care about those issues? The vision speech is not your wishes, hopes and dreams for the community. No, first you will ferret out facets of every single issue by finding out _who wants what and how they want you to get it._

If you are not sure who the Titans may be, go online or phone a city hall clerk to locate former candidates' campaign contribution lists, often they are posted online and always they will be open information. Clerks may request a few cents a page to copy the reports, but they cannot deny the lists exist or say a copy is not available.

If an opponent is the incumbent, get his/her campaign contributions for the last three reporting dates. Ask for the campaign reports for all the people who previously ran against the incumbent, or if you are running for an open seat, get the last three campaign reports for whoever was in the office you are seeking. Each report will have a name, address (but seldom the telephone number) of the previous contributors and the amount contributed.

Once you have secured campaign contribution reports and looked up all the phone numbers, it is time to make some calls. This is no time to be shy, information gathering telephone calls to the people listed on the previous campaign contributor lists and the person-to-person visits are expected. Not phoning the Titans and previous contributors would be, well, weird and comical in a political joke sort of way. Phone the people listed on the campaign reports and listen carefully to what they believe are their prime issues and more importantly, if they will tell, who is for or against their issues.

Make sure you have ample minutes on the cell phone, because in addition to the people on those campaign lists you also must meet with the public relations departments at your local Chamber of Commerce, Associated General Contractors, and all the unions and associations who represent fire, police, teachers, nurses, and local government employees.

In addition, contact and make appointments with the leadership of the Board of Realtors, AARP, retired government employees, the local phone and electrical company employees, and women's clubs and organizations.

Talk, but mostly listen to a principal from a poor neighborhood, Senior citizens during their free lunch at the Senior center, a few lobbyists and a successful person in a public office that is perceived as one-step higher than the office you are seeking.

Finally, make an appointment with the chairperson of the local Republican, Democratic and Libertarian offices to discuss their interpretation of the hot local issues. If you are not able to get an appointment with the Chair, try the office secretary. Secretaries are usually the most knowledgeable and agreeable person to discuss issues with. They usually cannot keep secrets—they will tell you everything if you are patient.

Following the Money (FTM)

YOUR JOB IS to be clever and ferret out the reality of local issues. The reality of a solution or a problem is not always, as it appears. Solutions are often open political secrets and often, those secrets meant to be kept to yourself. Palatable political danger is when you believe you have identified with absolute certainty, an obvious solution to a neighborhood problem—and then you find out, too late, you made the wrong assessment.

Where is the truth to why Titans run communities the way they do? Thorough review of an issue can bring in a troubling perspective: namely, the secret you are supposed to keep. You heard the community leader say one thing; however, you aren't sure you understood who, what, and why.

Ah, truth, it is in the eyes of the Titans. In other words, figure out who ultimately benefits financially from controversial projects. That means again, as a professional candidate, a large portion of your job is to figure out who is feeding at the public trough and what those pigs will eventually directly or indirectly ask you to do.

Questioning why the Titan is committed to a project or ideal is tricky. How in the world would a ruthless candidate know if a Titan's parent company has set their caps to build a depressed railroad track? How in the world would a newbie candidate know if the property on either side of the railroad tracks is contaminated and considered a Superfund site? How would anyone ever know if contaminated soil was dug up, hauled away and cleaned—or simply spread in gullies or under the new freeway expansion or left to bubble with PCE's under the newly built American Indian hospital?

What is mystifying to a newbie ruthless candidate is how sneaky the Titans are when protecting the real reason for their support of an issue. Understanding Titans and finding your personal campaign strategy depends on figuring out the schemes. Make sense of those schemes by following the money. **(FTM)**

For instance, you are positive that local arterial and neighborhood roads aren't being paved efficiently. You see the asphalt weeping in the cracks during the summer, and fraying potholes in the winter. Why, you ask, doesn't the city build roads in concrete? Is it because the companies that bid those road jobs are incompetent and do a lousy job?

No, they do a great job. The construction contractors are using asphalt instead of concrete because they own asphalt paving equipment and not concrete paving equipment. If the road contractor buys new concrete laying equipment, he would have to give up resurfacing and rebuilding the roads every five years.

★ **FTM** Asphalt is a recurring source of income—a cash cow—concrete roads are not. Moreover, resurfacing and rebuilding roads means a living wage, union wage or prevailing wage jobs for both union and non-union families.

Another instance, you may think the school district is slow to build new schools. The Titans want a convention center. The local general contractors would be happy about building either project. Would the community build a new convention center or school?

The convention center would be built first because there is a promise of conventioneers and new money flow into the community. The convention center is a venue built for the Titans' use—to increase hotel room nights, put on concerts and add to special events—the room taxes and additional revenue may add to the tax base. Oh, it's a redevelopment area? What a dilemma.

★ **FTM** Schools do not generate revenue. Yes, they may improve society—still they do not generate revenue—unless of course a school is the cornerstone of a housing development. New schools will be built when the voters get outraged. Until then, the school district can implement more busing across town or add year round schools to eliminate overcrowding.

Another example is flood control. The commercial developers, homebuilders and the local university have many thousands of acres of wetlands that are in the flood plain and they need 5-10 years to build out that wetland with homes and industrial buildings.

The United States Corps of Engineers is pressured by a Senator's office via powerful local Titans of commercial and homebuilders, along with their attorneys and a few unsuspecting university folks. There is an alliance coupled with an official sounding name, say, the Bruckee River Water Management Council.

The bogus but official sounding council hurriedly commissions a self-serving report that differs from the USGS report by advocating a 1/8 cent tax on the citizens, thereby eliminating financial responsibility of the landowners to ameliorate the flood plain.

★ **FTM** Figure out who wants to build out the housing project, finish the industrial park and or keep their grazing land and most importantly, who is on the bogus council. The people on the bogus official sounding council may be the Titans or their representatives who plan for the taxpayers to pay for flood mitigation—only after the Titans build out, in the flood plain, huge projects of additional industrial parks and homes.

Writing and the Delivery of the Vision Statement

WHEN YOU DELIVER the vision speech, you must show your integrity is impeccable and that you will do what you say. Consider Cicero of the Classic Age, (64 B.C.) who believed perceived reputation, positive qualities and a distinctive character persuades more than logic. In other words, people agree with people they trust—more than with bombproof logic.

Although Cicero ended his successful life as an orator by having his head and hands cut off by his enemies, (for good measure, Mark Antony's wife Fulvia stuck her hairpin in his tongue), who cares, that's then, this is now: and besides with unremitting practice, cunning and ruthlessness you shouldn't have fear of reprisal.

Mull over the following list combining Cicero, Retired Judge Bob Coates of San Diego and my suggestions on how to formulate, write and deliver your vision speech to reinforce a connection with your voters.

Cicero, Coates and I agree: we favor flattery, remembering voters names, to always be humble and human, to master the art of a deep gaze into the eyes of voters and seldom waste time, except with people who are apparent centers of influence and perhaps most important of all: **always offer hope.**

- ★ Use the proper language for your audience
- ★ Use clarity so that even the least informed understands your concepts
- ★ Make sure your anecdotes employ the sensibilities of the audience
- ★ Make super sure the words you speak fit the audience; no sexist terms, vague anachronisms or PC language that may leave your audience scratching their heads in bewilderment.
- ★ Your tone or your voice and gestures, along with short jerky sentences will kill you. Notice how Politicians talk and talk and talk—

★ Stage your tone: speak in a normal conversation speech at first (expressing your character), then turn up your voice (deliver your argument) and then near the end make the voice volume go way up (get emotional).

★ Get your eye mojo down pat. Cicero was the first to tell us that the eyes are windows to the soul. I suggest you watch former President Ronald Reagan speak to a crowd.

★ Right now it is all about the voter and campaign contributors. Stick to what the voters want, *not* what the voters need.

★ Figure out what people want to hear and tell them exactly that. Do not give plausible solutions until you know what the Titans want.

★ Your reason for running is not a list of your angers, your dreams, your hopes or your aspirations. It is all about them: the voters and the Titans.

Keep in mind that old solutions must be regenerated, (in order to keep those who thought of the old ideas and implemented the solutions are on your side), then add a little bit of an acceptable solution, along with some hint of change that is perceived as a sensible, albeit enhanced solution.

After developing the problems and solutions that are on the top of voters' minds, you still have to be an expert on other issues: review local ideas about building big box stores, repairing potholes, controlling crime, eliminating graffiti, illegal immigration, cellular towers, all-day kindergarten, ambulance service, airport noise, dust control, zoning, government pay and benefit packages, open meeting laws, speed limits, building codes, parks and recreation, theater productions, Christmas tree disposal, a public Menorah, the poor and the homeless, bus routes, taxes, and public school issues.

From the problems and solutions, discussed with the Titans, select three you are willing to make the cornerstone of the campaign. Now that you know more than you need to know about almost all the issues: (both the problems and solutions) you are ready to write and practice the vision speech.

Write three versions of the vision statement: a short (1 minute), medium (3 minute) and long version (5 minutes). Commit to memory the basics on all three but especially the first two. Practice with both your radio voice and your TV face and voice. Tape and time yourself.

Remember, do not memorize the vision speech word for word—the more memorized and polished it is, the cornier and more canned you will sound. You should sound natural, like you, but like the best version of you. The only way to achieve the natural tone is practice, practice and then practice some more, on the way to your weekly Toastmasters meeting.

Most debates and radio interviews begin with a one-minute introduction and vision speech. Inside that one minute, it is your responsibility to your supporters to include and act with the following style:

Vision—show the voter a positive mental image.

Nurture—show the voter the attitude you will have when contemplating the issues.

Solve the problems—for the town or board.

Regenerate—new old ideas with new thinking to achieve previously thwarted projects.

Demonstrate—the ability to use positive interaction within a potentially hostile community atmosphere by using your communication skills to show how you will cooperate within the entire community.

Just in case you still do not have a clue about the vision thing, I want to hold your hand and show you a few emblematic problems of the typical 21ˢᵗ century community. These problems and the solutions are descriptive enough to make a Titan smile and bob their head in agreement.

You want to assure the voters that you will get things done in a simple and commonsense way. Here are some neighborhood problems commonly found in small-to-medium communities. We have included a descriptive adjective and a vague, but sensible solution.

COMMUNITY PROBLEM	EMOTIONAL WORDS THAT SHOW YOU SHARE THEIR PAIN	IDEAS FOR SOLUTIONS "LET ME KNOW—DOES THIS SEEM LIKE A SOLUTION YOU COULD SUPPORT?"
POTHOLES IN NEIGHBORHOOD RESIDENTIAL ROADS	Bumpy, unsightly neighborhood roads, lower home values	Pothole hotline 333-5555 put on all community vehicles.
GANGS, DRIVE BY SHOOTINGS, GRAFFITI	Lowered home values, neighborhoods scared, Children cannot play outside	Community Policing, After school programs, Graffiti hot line telephone number, neighborhood forums and town hall meetings
DOMESTIC VIOLENCE, HOMELESS WOMEN, AND CHILDREN WITH ALCOHOL OR DRUG DEPENDENCY	Schools and classrooms affected—children often hungry and emotionally frail	Family Court established just for women and children, Safe houses, Drug/ Alcohol rehab
BUDGET SHORTFALLS, SMALL COMMUNITY SCHOOL BOARDS (LEGISLATIVELY REVIEWED)	Look where our hard earned tax dollars are going! Our money is being thrown down the drain. We love our town; let's show the state we can do better.	How about, we create a citizen audit committee, establish baselines, then if we win with those ideas let's push for a line item veto! Our elected officials must be held accountable.

ECONOMIC DIVERSIFICATION	Everyone in the community wins with new companies coming to town.	We all want higher paying jobs and prosperity, so let's make sure the "powers that be" know we want to go after clean industry first.
INCREASE REVENUE BY INCREASING SALES TAXES	Everyone knows that the last resort is to increase sales tax. It's a regressive tax and I oppose sales tax increases when we are all suffering. We need to increase our revenue but not on the backs of our citizens.	That said, if we can save one of our Seniors from hunger or loneliness by building (or improving) a Senior center...if we can keep our youth busy and happy with new ballparks and an indoor recreation center, or develop vocational job centers—then I could see the merit. DO NOT SAY YOU WILL RAISE TAXES OR ARE IN FAVOR OF RAISING TAXES.
GROWTH BUILDING APARTMENTS INDUSTRIAL COMMERCIAL	Our roads will be clogged with traffic, our schools full to the brim. The community revenue stream from taxes can/cannot take the strain of new growth only if we plan.	I say we establish "Smart Growth"—let's camouflage big box stores with both extensive landscaping and attractive architecture
ENVIRONMENT	We must commit to the preservation of our local history while embracing the need for new innovative ways to raise revenue with an increase of taxes.	Historic buildings may be the way to increase tourism that will help our community with new dollars from the outside. Let's put new facades on the buildings, sandblast the sidewalks, add some public art and find new pride in our community.

JAILS FULL	Tough on crime... increase Police presence and use a common sense approach for our judges and courts.	We could use the court fees or parking meter revenue to establish boot camps, church-run community service and job training instead of jail time. The entire community needs to step up to the idea that we must change our idea of "jail time"
PROPERTY TAXES	I worry so for Seniors and people on fixed income losing homes from the inability to pay the mounting debt from property taxes. We must find a solution to this problem.	Many people have asked me to investigate how Calif. Prop 13 was introduced to the legislators. We must find a new direction to increase our revenue stream and protect our most treasured citizens.
SENIOR CITIZENS	Why don't we ask them what they want and need to improve their quality of life and maintain their dignity?	We must ask ourselves, are we giving our Seniors the dignity they deserve? Do they need more Police protection, improved transportation, housing and utilities ombudsmen to work with local community leaders?
ARTS AND CULTURE	You already know we don't have a symphony or a museum, and have only a few traveling art exhibits coming through our town. Is this enough music and culture for our families?	Arts and culture come with a pride in our community. Let's look at starting with a special event, say something for the Fourth of July. How about an old-fashioned parade celebrating our teachers, firefighters and Police?

RECREATION	It's a shame we don't have enough places students and young people from 12 to 17 can meet and have some old-fashioned fun.	Let's commit ourselves to finding funds and approaching the local school district on ways we can make every school a weekend—and summer—recreation center for the whole family. We not only create summer jobs for our teens, but also keep our kids on the right track.

All right, you've picked three issues the constituents are passionate about, now pick three issues the Titans demand you be passionate about, and finally pick three issues that cause union membership to cheer after they listen to your vision speech. The primary reason to be an expert on at least 9 or more issues is to be prepared for the editorial boards, union bosses and the Men's and Women's fraternal clubs.

Sometimes these groups will send out a questionnaire in advance but often they don't. The meetings are mandatory so you had better be well informed of their problems, concerns, and an understanding of how they want their problems fixed.

Bear in mind, they don't really want to know how you want to fix an issue—they want to know if you know how they want their problem fixed.

Editorial Boards and Contractor Union Sample Questions

★ Can you name any taxes you would re-examine or repeal?
★ Is the war on drugs succeeding in our town?

★ Do you think residents of our town should have the right to carry a concealed firearm?

★ What is your position on Eminent Domain?

★ Do you approve or disapprove of the downtown redevelopment area expansion?

★ Do you approve of the expansion of the ballparks and recreation areas in the Northwest?

★ Do you know any union members?

★ What is your position on open negotiations?

★ Explain your understanding of minimum wage, living wage and prevailing wage.

★ Where do you stand on two, three and four year cost of living contracts?

Firefighter and Police Union Sample Questions

★ Why are you running for office?

★ What are your political aspirations?

★ What is your position on collective bargaining?

★ Would you support legislation to restrict mandatory topics of bargaining?

★ What is your position on the privatization of police services/ Firefighting?

★ What is your position on civilian review boards?

★ What is your opinion on Firefighters holding ENT licenses?

★ What is your position on marijuana?

★ How many gang related deaths were in our city last year; is the Police department handling the situation correctly?

★ What is your opinion on community policing?

★ What is your stand on automatic weapons?

★ What is your position on 'sneak and peek'?

★ How should the immigration laws be enforced?

Women's Club Sample Questions

★ What one challenge have you had while getting where you have today and how have you overcome it?
★ What advice would you give to girls and young women about the political world?
★ What is something you now know that you wished you'd know when you were young enough to be a Brownie or Girl Scout?
★ What advice would you give girls and young women about the working world?
★ What did you want to be when you grew up?
★ Who is a woman you admire and why?
★ What is the best advice you were ever given?
★ What is one thing you want to accomplish this year and next year?
★ What book have you read lately?

I realize that gives you more than nine issues and I said there would be only three. Yes, you must be familiar with many issues thoroughly and consider the solutions too. Nevertheless, only three issues are yours and therein lays the tough part. You will have to juggle all nine issues and discern which ones are central to the firefighters, the union bosses, the clubs and the Chamber of Commerce.

Mistakes are not allowed. Once you make a mistake about an issue, usually you cannot take it back gracefully. That is why eloquently discussing issues and the right answers for the appropriate audiences is what makes a well-informed ruthless political panderer.

Write the vision speeches and practice, all of them. Remember, a solution too specific may turn the voters who want a different solution against you. Be vague but helpful. Be sensible, deliberate but never specific. You must pretend as if your vision speech is about your hopes and dreams for the community, in reality, you now should understand the game; it's a whole lot about the Titans and you are along for the ride.

That is why I cannot emphasize enough; know the issues and what you stand for and who is standing with you. Don't you dare look blankly and stutter pathetically," *I want to give back to the community."*

I like the following vision speeches. They both introduce the candidate and explain what is wrong in the community and how she has the qualifications and desire to fix the problems. These are real life honest to goodness reasons for running, vision statements, women have used to win.

★ "I'm well-educated, child-centered and love Kansas. My name is Michelle Neary. I have been a proud member of our community for twenty years and have chosen to raise my three girls here, too. As a mother, teacher, cancer survivor and your neighbor, I recognize that we need strong representation in the State Assembly. I have the business sense and common sense to get the job done in our capital. Keeping Kansas a good place to live, work and raise a family, now and for our children, is my top priority."

★ I am running for City Council because I was encouraged to do so by people in the neighborhoods who want a voice on the City Council. I want to be that voice. If you elect me to the Reno City Council, I'll be a forceful advocate for community pride and redevelopment. I'll fight to make sure that every penny is spent with the optimum of fiscal responsibility. I'll fight to bring the prosperity of our new economy to all our citizens. I'll fight for regional Smart Growth, while insuring more open space, more community centers and more parks. It is my willingness to fight hard on these issues that has the allies of the incumbent City Council so worried.

★ Hi, I'm Fay, a lifelong Alaskan blessed with a wonderful husband, three children and two grandchildren. Like you, I care about our future. As a business owner, realtor and insurance agent who has worked in ranching and construction, I'm uniquely qualified to satisfy the demands of this job. I've always been committed to our community, and I want to continue that work as your mayor. I am confident I possess the leadership skills and experience to be effective. Most of all, I have an ability to bring people together and get things done.

★ I am running for city council because I have the vision and the experience to guide our town in a direction that benefits us all. I will make Pleasantville a place where people can start a business without excessive government bureaucracy. Our schools must be responsive to the needs of students and the community, and schools must be accountable for their results. Pleasantville is my home and I will work hard as your city council person to provide the leadership Pleasantville needs. I believe the people of Pleasantville are entitled to a council member with a commitment to public service and accountability to the taxpayers. The job of a council member is to see that the business of the City is done in a timely and cost-effective manner. As a business owner and attorney for ten years, I understand the need to provide a high level of service by eliminating wasteful spending. I promise to run our city government the same way.

★ North Southpaw is growing rapidly, and so are the challenges that face us as we work to keep our community a place we can all be proud of. This is our home, and you and I have invested in it with our hearts and souls. We need hardworking, dedicated and accountable representatives who listen to your concerns. We must find the underlying cause of the money Manhattan Steel Corporation owes our town. I promise to work hard every day to ensure a more secure tomorrow. (Of course, she has already talked to the plant owner and realizes the Titans have come to a compromise with the county on the past due bill. No candidate attacks the major town business without first going behind closed doors and talking over what is acceptable to say to the voters.)

You may think, that clearing what you say with the Titans sounds a little sneaky and phony. Did I stutter when I told you earlier that politicians are often phony to the core? The key is consistency and the adaption of both Cicero and the Honorable Bob Coates rules of communication.

Soft Pandering

YOU TELL DIFFERENT audiences different vision statements. Adapting to your audience is the key to likability. That said, whether speaking to people gathered by the Chamber of Commerce or the Little League organizers of Yucaipa, the issues do not change—the vision is simply modified by the adaption of your tone, your language and your delivery.

Then after finding a connection with diction, recognize when it may be appropriate to place both hands in prayer mode as a final thank you or a right hand across the heart with a slight tilt of the head and eyes cast downward in order to make final connections with the audience.

Knowing who is in the audience tells you who is interested in your response to the issues, they want to see how you perform under pressure, *and* are interested in your candidacy There are different categories within male and female audiences. It is imperative to peruse the audience—or, if possible, to research them beforehand—and to be able to identify by sight—Titans and the issues they support.

Be hyper aware of your language style, innuendos, music and pop culture references or curses. The modification of your vision speech must be generational and gender-specific. Know your audience, and know how intimate you can be with them. Consider the age of the audience—mentioning that you will never forget where you were when John F. Kennedy was assassinated or where you were when Apollo 11 landed on the moon, will lose a young audience.

Hard Core Pandering

GROUPS OF MEN, **Seniors and Rural** voters are specific demographics who demand a special concocted candidate style. Don't be phony with Seniors or the membership of a Men's club. Don't laugh or smile too much. Both groups like to be wooed into a feeling of empowerment. But they won't give you a hint what it is that they want from you.

Collectively, they seem to relish the idea that their votes count a lot more than others. It's a crapshoot when you attend and perform to Seniors only or at Men's fraternal clubs. Tell them whatever they want to hear if you can figure out what that might be. I don't know why these two groups are the way they are. Both groups demand that you be polite, that I am sure of, and to be natural, charming, bright and friendly. They may react to your vision speech like a pack of wolves, or worse, ignore you, doodle on their napkins and clap politely when you are done.

Men's club audiences are a stubborn lot. I know of what I speak, they are a mixed bag of heard-it-all curmudgeons and enthusiastic new members: neither type of member really cares about the vision speech. Normally, the focus is only on their projects, their club and their unyielding position on community issues. Some, with bossy wives or successful daughters, may show you they like you with a firm handshake, a wink or a nod—seldom will you notice any one member clapping louder than the rest.

Simply being a woman will raise the red flag of incompetence; making it fly higher are the wrong selections of clothing, a shrill instead of modulated deep voice and being ignorant, immature and nervously giggly while giving the vision speech. The key to success with any group of people is to know when to add the charm.

The late Lady Diana was good at being charming and it may work for you. Her technique was to tilt her head down slightly and look up through her eyelashes. If you can perfect this technique, men, who may have already decided they don't like you or your vision—may change their minds and see at you as prey.

Just as important, to make believe you are prey—is to openly admit that you aren't the favorite candidate. Instead of fighting the tide, give them endearing admiration. "I know I am not one of...your people... (tilt, look up through your lashes)...but what I do know about you is—you have built and support the finest Boys and Girls club in the state. You know, (look them straight in the eye) you are a club I'd be proud to support..."

Every club or service meeting has different rules for candidate introductions; most of the time you will not get the chance to take the podium and give your vision speech. And if the plan is to be introduced by the President or a member of a service club, forget it—introductions often costs upwards of $100 to introduce a candidate. So, instead, work the room—meet every person individually instead of a mass introduction.

The best way to work any room is to have a handler or better yet, a club member bring you to every table, they don't hold your hand; but he/she does rescue you from a long winded discussion; by touching your elbow and propelling you towards the next person, next table or out of the venue.

I AM WELL AWARE THAT TO STEREOTYPE Rurals or Seniors is asking for trouble. It is not nice to be overtly ageist or sexist. Rurals and Seniors seldom contribute money or time to your campaign, but they always vote. Therefore, if you slight Seniors or a Ruralist— in any way, by ignoring their ideas or forgetting that it's all about them—you're asking for big trouble.

Both groups gossip among themselves. Both groups have their own newspapers and newsletters that will or won't endorse you. It's a crapshoot.

One key to a Senior audience is to promise any extra cash will be diverted to a Senior Center. Even the rich ones love the notions of reduction in property taxes, free or special rides on buses or taxis, reduced rates for telephones, electricity and discounts at civic events.

Seniors are often suspicious of early voting and, as such, do not much cotton to early voting. More often than not, they fill out absentee ballots. Catering to Seniors by contacting them one on one and listening to their complaints and suggestions before they send in their absentee vote is an imperative.

Another very trite ploy to getting the Senior vote is to identify and latch on to the coattails of a handsome and/or well-known and well-liked male candidate that is running for an up ticket office. (Up ticket is usually Federal or State offices, down ticket are local offices—the down ticket refers to the placement on the ballot.) Senior women aren't dead, they appreciate good looking male candidates; if you follow the up ticket male candidates each time they attend a Senior event you may win the Senior women's vote.

Finally, recognize that you can't really fool around with Seniors; they don't always get jokes, you have to speak slowly and loudly to be heard and understood. It is a real trick to find the pitch and tone of voice, which makes you both friendly and professional, without sounding condescending.

Since I had the nerve to tackle ageism and sexism, now let us glance over at the Rural voter. The only thing remotely stereotypical about the Ruralist may be the occasional beer belly. These men and women are the grit of our communities. They are a hardworking lot. Never give a Rural a limp handshake: prepare for the pain—they have arms and hands of steel.

Many Ruralists are college or university graduates that chose to live in the hinterlands. The ruthless candidate must always look straight into their eyes and be forewarned: when introduced, never ever attempt to hug or dip into a double air kiss greeting.

A Ruralist is often a white, conservative Republican and may be at odds with city folk. They do not see why poor folk, if they happen to be hungry or cold, don't grow some food or make some warmer clothes. For the Ruralist, government is less visible—so they don't get all the hoopla of cutting down the size of government. Although there is always an exception to the idea that less is best: often a Ruralist would like funds to crack down on the meth labs just outside of town.

In the meantime, use care if you are wishin' and hopin' to connect with the Ruralists while you put on your country gal façade, need I remind you to be real in front of the audience? Although we both know the "real you" does vary a tad.

★ 44 ★

WOMEN'S GROUPS ARE THE SPANKING MACHINE OF POLITICS. Court them with all your talent and might. It is illogical, but for any little reason they do not like you, they can and will destroy the campaign.

There are many reasons why we women act bored or stop listening. I heard somewhere that one reason we women do not listen is that we can think much faster than anyone can talk. Sometimes the audience wants you to shut up and they want to talk. If you sense restlessness, stop, reword your statment and ask for a question.

Not to belabor the point, but, when women do not connect it is campaign devastation. Bitchy women can and will damage your reputation and create little fictions that can grow into ideological zealotry—conversely if they adore you with unflinching zealous idolatry you can count on them staying all the way to the ballot box with you.

Even the evil ones will be the best listeners, motivators, networkers and multi-taskers, plus they are usually more focused, empathic and tenacious than men. If you connect with women, you will be in high clover—three to five dedicated women can run a campaign with perfection.

Conversely, be forewarned, female volunteers for the opposition candidates are beyond evil. By evil, tenacious and motivated, I mean they can and will try to make you cry if they find a flaw in your reasoning, wardrobe or hairdo. I am thinking of Carly Fiorina's friends' cattiness about Senator Barbara Boxers' hairdo, "G-d, what is that hair? It's So-o-o yesterday."

No matter the audience, Women, Men, Senior or Rural, up on the stage, dais or while working the room, every voter must feel they already know you. From the moment they see you, they make assumptions. As you introduce yourself and describe your vision to these wonderful voting blocks, they seem to immediately decide, sometimes altogether, like a locust swarm, if you are one of them or not.

You may or may not be one of them—but that does not mean you don't try to find at least one similarity and emulate that similar trait. Pay attention to the "normative" behaviors of the group you are wooing. If they all have a martini in hand—put one in your hand too; if they are all drinking beer out of the can or bottle—do the same. If they speak with an east coast nasal or a southern accent feign a little and if they are mostly wearing crosses; pull yours out.

While we are talking about diverse audiences, if the name of the club or organization has Rainbow, Log Cabin or the letters PFLAG (Parents, Friends of Lesbians, and Gays) as catch phrases in their literature or on their web site—you can be sure your audience will be family members and/or Gay, Bi and/or Transsexual people.

Really, orientation should make no difference, except if one of your platform planks is traditional marriage or your religion denies the rights of gays and lesbians to exist. You shouldn't be using language that is offensive to certain groups anyway.

Always use gender-neutral language and be gracious to everyone you meet. Robin Abrahams, author and *Boston Globe Magazine* columnist, thinks like you and I do; our world is in flux: what with everyone coming into full equality. She reminds us in her 2009, *Miss Conduct's Mind of Manners*. "Everyone is not straight…; and… nearly everyone wants to be respected in the public sphere… and almost all of us want a chance at life with someone who will love, honor and cherish us." I think you should skirt gay issues or use pro language.

The assembling of a political campaign closely resembles the Buddhist parable of the blind men describing an elephant. One blind man feels the tusks, another blind man touches the soft, flexible ear, and a third imagines in his mind's eye the massive strength of the beast just from holding the leg. Each of the blind men experiences the elephant in his own perspective—and yet not one of them can understand the whole beast.

For the newbie candidate a political campaign, both you and the campaign, resembles the Buddhist elephant parable; no question, a political campaign and the ruthless woman candidate are multi-faceted, full of experiences and chock full of deliberate tasks that don't seem to jibe with the glamorous ideas and TV mini clips of smiling, handshaking, baby kissing politicians.

By now, everyone close to you is sick of talking about the run for office, you are clear on the secret, non-spoken personal reason for running for office, you have examined almost all of your limitations and negatives and formed a plausible short explanation for each of those negatives. You know the community issues and the complicated solutions and you can communicate to both the voters and the Titans why you are better suited than any other candidate to represent them in public office.

The Candidate Uniform is What Separates the Winners from the Losers

TO WIN AT all costs is to be a vision of political perfection. You know something is right when people sidle up near and are eager to be your friend. Just like finding the issues and solutions and giving a flawless vision speech, it is your duty to emulate the political fashion sense of a successful women candidate. I want you to dress as the clone of a well-loved and successful political woman. Look everywhere in your town, city, or state—for a woman politician who has a similar body type as yours.

Then before, you decide on an ensemble, you have to do some legwork. Cruise the neighborhoods where your voters live. What are the basic socioeconomics of your constituents? Are the homes large with pastures and animals out back? Are there old rusty vehicles sitting in the driveways? Are the voters living close together in mobile home parks, condominiums or apartments? The candidate uniform depends on the demographics of the target constituents and the candidate uniform can vary from precinct to precinct.

The candidate uniform is a fundamental clothing decision that must shout, *"I'm sincere and sexy but I'm professional."* A choice of the kitten heels, the burgundy pumps or the cowboy boots are now a responsibility and maybe even an unstated contractual obligation between you, the Titans and the voters.

You don't want voters, seeing you in a soccer mom ensemble or looking haggard in baggy jeans, an oversized monogrammed t-shirt and clip-on costume jewelry, raise their eyebrows in surprise and say in disbelief, "Oh, you're running for office?"

The candidate uniform is the visible signifier of societal worth and position. You must never appear fragile, fat, weak, misguided or disheveled. Your job is to give the illusion that you are just a tad better dressed than the voters you meet.

Why? Because the ultimate candidate uniform goal is for voters to tell other voters: "Gee, she really looks like a councilwoman, mayor, county supervisor, borough president, school board member, water district board member, superintendent, commissioner, Parent Teacher Association president, Little League president. "

You absolutely must be recognized the minute you walk into a business, office or social engagement. Use a conservative fashion sense, and keep in mind that when tired, distraught by some bad press or in a hurry, you may slip up and wear something "un-candidate-like." Such a blunder may cost votes. That is why when I say put together 4-6 outfits, really; I am serious.

There are other sane reasons to show up to every function perfectly dressed in a candidate uniform. First, confidence soars when you are impeccably dressed, and second, as the months go on and on, you will be so weary that reaching for a designated candidate uniform—will eliminate a wardrobe malfunction.

The public will accept professional and feminine with a wisp of bitchiness and a hint of manly. It is possible to go overboard on the bitchy feminine and end up what could be read as mannish. Sadly, in our phallocentric and heterosexist society, this will not get votes.

Whaaat?" "I'm supposed to wear a successful candidate uniform that's crisp, clean and approachable, feminine and somewhat bitchy?" Think a little bit bitchy, as looking a little bit country: two inch hoop earrings or red shoes with a black suit; a pair of kitten heeled shoes or upper calf, tight-fitting black high heel boots will keep the men looking and listening and the women wondering if that style would look good on them.

I think the perfect candidate uniform to wear to impress Titans is a St. John classic suit. Go online and find a department store that sells St. John, select a matching jacket, skirt and pants. Make sure the jacket neckline accommodates a complementary silk blouse, and/ or a scarf. Buy a gold or silver knit tank for evening. On this ensemble, including the extra blouses, scarves and shoes, you may spend around $4,500.

Or, if you have a consignment store like Blythe Anderson's 'Labels' in Reno, Nevada, you may find the perfect slightly worn, St. John ensemble, nearly new, for around $2,000. Blythe supports women's issues. Mention my name, Blythe or Robbie will give you a great deal. 'Labels' is open seven days a week. (775) 825-6000. A St. John investment will carry you to meetings and special occasions for the rest of your life. The two great things about a St. John: you can plump up or slim down because a St. John is a knit and they never go out of style. The Titans' wives will be surprised and impressed by classic style.

In most states, you can write off your candidate uniform as a campaign expense, so consider the wardrobe investment as a loan to your campaign. When the donations start rolling in, pay the campaign coffers back for the expense. **ALWAYS** check your state laws on campaign wardrobe expenses and be careful, I know of a candidate that nearly went to jail for using campaign contributions to have her nails done and to buy campaign uniforms.

Now, to dress up or down for voters, you have to know what those people think is appropriate attire. That is why I said to cruise your precinct neighborhoods. You are perceptive enough to know that cowboy boots at a beachside mobile home park is not relating to your voter, but large houses with farm animals grazing in the back forty may find those boots charming and well, normal.

For a late winter-late spring primary find in your closet or buy all weather black wool pants, one each Ralph Lauren black, cream and deep blue turtlenecks, a pair of gold moderate hoop earrings and two great quality jackets: both in jewel tones: one in Chinese red and the other in a sapphire blue. Don't be afraid of color, it is the key to being noticed—I mean the jacket and blouse, not the pants or skirt. Keep the bottom half of your body in black, brown or beige and the jacket vibrant with color and style. Try not to wear all red, all black, or all white.

If you live in a more temperate or subtropical latitude with warm winters and spring; try similar fashion ideas—with a lot of rayon or polyester mix—you don't want to look crumply on a humid afternoon.

If you purchase new ensembles, don't wander through the department store trying to create the look by mix and matching. Buy all the pieces at the same time, made by the same designer.

A double or triple strand of fake pearls works very well too. Make sure they are knotted between each pearl; no one can ever know they are not real. Add to your ensembles a very expensive looking watch, vintage works.

The final emphasis of the candidate uniform is a belt with a great big, beautiful buckle. Big belt buckles suggest power. If you are a National Rifle Association (NRA) member, order the dual metal fancy buckle; it's about $125. It's gorgeous and all the NRA members will know you are one of them and vote for you. Or, if you don't have an affinity to guns, have a belt buckle made that represents a devotion to your community and/or the community logo. You should almost never take your jacket off, so don't worry about looking fat with a belt cinching in your waist.

I like tattoos but your voters may not—if you are in Seattle, for instance, go for it. In the interest of proving maturity and knowledge of decorum, I suggest you cover your tattoos and take out the nose diamond, and encourage the eyebrow double hole barbell to fill in with regular dabs of salve.

There are always exceptions to the rules: the only time the tattoos and piercing should ever show is when you are on a university campus. For goodness sake don't go from campus to Rotary club and forget to use cover up and/or take them out.

If you are grown up and gutsy enough to run for public office, the days of making a statement with platinum blonde hair, Burning Man dreadlocks, braless jiggling, faint nipple ridges showing through your sweater or blouse, eyebrow barbells and lip hoops are long over. Yes, even in the privacy of your own home. You never know when the Channel Two TV anchor will come knocking on your front door rummaging for a human-interest story.

Sometimes, you will be tempted to wear an animal print. Do not wear them at the PETA or local zoo board of trustees' annual meeting. To the contrary, shoes in animal print with a black or brown dress can be part of your bitchy side. A faux animal print coat over a simple dress is probably ok, too. Bottom line: when there is any doubt, just don't wear faux fur or animal prints. And most certainly keep the real furs and reptile skin boots at the very, very back of your closet.

You may have noticed many women candidates and office holders have repositioned jacket buttons. Get a tailor to find the sweet spot. Congresswoman Nancy Pelosi's fitted jackets often close at the first button, positioned directly under the bosom. Repositioning of the button to this position exaggerates the smallest part of the torso.

I have also noticed that many candidates will modify suit jackets by repositioning a traditional style lapel upward instead of it laying flat down the chest. Pushing the lapels upwards creates a Nehru style that also leads the voters' eye upwards. Another low cost trick is to change plastic buttons to brass. Simple brass buttons transform a blasé jacket to a double-breasted signature of power and military authority.

Old-fashioned male etiquette was to seldom take off a suit jacket. Men use to ask women, if it was all right to take off their jackets. I agree that that old-fashioned notion also goes for women candidates. Never take off a jacket and get comfortable. You are the candidate. There is no time to be comfortable.

Nice shoes, appropriate to the occasion and to the style of an ensemble, are essential to a well-dressed candidate. Buy the most expensive and comfortable shoe you can afford. Shoes *must* be comfortable; on the other hand, no one should ever sidle up to you and say:

"BOY, THOSE SHOES LOOK COMFORTABLE," OR
"HOW DO YOU WALK IN THOSE?"

What about undergarments? Molded cup bras are pricey and but worth the costs; with a molded helmet covering your nipples, you will never unintentionally or pointedly tell the audience, "It's cold in here." Who doesn't know a tight girdle pushes up our middle-earth waist fat, which then causes a muffin top? There is a debate: which is worse, muffin top or lumpy back fat. Both may be camouflaged by wearing either a well-fitted, soft material unbuttoned jacket or a full or half-body stretchy spandex foundation.

As a post-menopausal woman, when you wear spandex, you will probably sweat. Unless the temperature is near 60 degrees, with no more than 10% humidity, be pre- pared to seep around the edges, eventually you may be waving a napkin and asking, *"Is it hot in here or is it me?"* Most voters are suspicious of post- menopausal women, especially when they are holding a portable fan or waving a nap- kin desperate to find a cool breeze.

NEVER WEAR

1. Any shoe with an ankle strap
2. Severe pointed toe shoes
3. Stacked heels
4. Loafers with a dress
5. Oxfords
6. Sandals with sparkles
7. Flip flops
8. White tennis shoes
9. Black tennis shoes
10. Dirty, scuffed, or worn out shoes

Excess weight can be a problem too. If your BMI is over 34, consider going on a diet. More than likely, if you are overweight, nothing will hide your muffin top and back fat. Voters and Titans usually avoid fat women candidates. If you are unattractively fat, don't go in public much, do a lot of radio, and mail out your bro- chures with a great head-shot. When caught in public, stand behind a group of children. No matter, if you are moribund obese, you must have a handsome, cute, pretty or beautiful face.

On the campaign trail there is no time to be tired or G-d forbid, look tired. Without some eye makeup, foundation and lipstick you'll look worn-out instead of radiant. Perfect your makeup by select- ing a foundation that is exactly the same color as your complexion. Don't skimp on this purchase, Dior's' Dior Nude face makeup will give your skin a flawless velvet sheen, so will Mary Kay products.

I am not a makeup maven; thousands of dollars of my department store and drugstore mistakes are in the back of my makeup drawer and in a shoebox under the bathroom sink. The sensible alternative to costly makeup mistakes is to go online to www.cosmeticscop. com and buy Paula Begoun's 6th edition of *Don't go to the Cosmetics Counter without Me.* Recently Begoun was a guest on the Dr. Oz show, she knows makeup—and I love and trust Dr. Oz—I say that we should follow his and her advice.

Seldom will you meet a candidate without a defined mouth. Messy or ugly lips are very unbecoming. Find a tinted lipstick and reapply it often. Tints and stains have a nice feel to them and will give lips a nice hint of color. The bonus of a lip tint is the gooey-ness. When you get tongue-tied and dry-mouthed a lip tint will help keep the upper and lower lip corners from getting dry and sticking together. Lips that stick together are a telltale sign of nervousness.

I remember an afternoon, on the campaign trail. My brother, Jim, (my other brother Randy died of AIDS in the 80's, that's why I advised you to be careful about the gay audiences) turned to me, at least fifteen minutes into a meet and greet and whispered, "Whoa, Baby Jane, what's up with the lips?" What, I thought, is he talking about? I fled to the nearest bathroom, looked into the mirror, to see dark lipstick way outside the natural lines, top and bottom.

Lipstick or lip stain must fit easily in your jacket pocket, cosmetic kit or inside your bra near your underarm. The smaller the lipstick or stain tube, the better, since you seldom will carry a purse. Don't put your lipstick in a pant pocket. The pocket may pooch out and make you look hippy. Sew all your pants pockets down so as not to be tempted to use them.

Speaking of mouths, mouth breathing is forbidden on the campaign trail, and there is no need to show teeth with every smile. You don't want to eat them; you just want them to love you enough to vote for you because they can plainly see you care about their hopes, wishes and dreams. Dare I mention a George Orwell observation: "You can have an affection for a murderer or a sodomite, but you cannot have an affection for a (wo)man whose breath stinks."

The eyes must always have a friendly smile. Never wear your tinted prescription glasses during conversations with voters. If they cannot see your eyes, they may misunderstand. Who doesn't know that eyeglasses should fit perfectly and harmonize with hair and face shapes? There are very few things sillier looking than an ill-fitting pair of eyeglasses, especially when askew.

Always wear mascara on your top lashes. If you tend to get weepy, about an animal project, or feel misunderstood, as Mrs. Clinton did during her Presidential campaign, use waterproof mascara. A positive little weep with one or two tears, either welled up or in one stream down the cheek, can go a long way (as long as they are not pre-menopausal tears). Avoid wearing false eyelashes, instead, try *Latisse,* the eyelash growth enhancement, it truly works.

When you are looking for a simple but chic hairstyle, be clear that the most important detail of your do, is that you must look put-together. A ruthless candidate knows that to have a bad hair day is to lose voters' faith. It is so trivial; but a bad or an old-fashioned do is cause for voters to consider your core may be old-fashioned and not in lockstep with their way of thinking.

Although Calista Gingrich was not a candidate, her hair has been one of the most talked about do's since Hillary Clintons' headbands. Hair, it seems, is an extension of a candidates' self and is always fair game for ridicule or review; remember, even a price of haircut can make news.

If you are sporting a helmet head or bubble hairdo, throw away your Aqua Net hair spray and check out the Bumble and Bumble counter for some mud or control paste, or consider my friend Veda's favorite—ICE's spray adhesive "BLAST." Lastly, let the mullet, the shaved-up-the-neck bowl cut, or the Mohawk grow out.

For functionality, I suggest a hairdo that permits you to wash your hair every two or three days. You don't want to blow out a 'do at 9AM and have it frizz on you just as you enter the Veterans of Foreign Wars annual Fourth of July function at 10AM.

If you color at home, be aware that newly applied hair color has a funky smell. Make sure that after coloring you hair at home double wash and condition with strongly scented products.

Do not overlook the grey or natural hair color sprouting out of a circular crown cowlick or at the temples. Buy tinted root coverage to use on the temples, hairline, crown and your mid part. Try 'Tween Time' by Roux or Bumble or Bumble Hair Powder. Both products are moderately priced at drugstores and/or salons.

Wind is a mortal enemy of the candidate with grey or dark roots. If there is a Santa Ana or a Nor'easter, be sure to wind check your hair. If your roots are showing, create a root-comb-over. Part your hair and rat it just a little—then make a "zigzagged" part and secure with some hair spray.

And while you and I are getting this personal, I want to speak frankly about facial hair, eyebrows and mustaches. In this day and age, it is ridiculous for any woman to have a mustache, hairs on her chin or sport a unibrow. Make a standing appointment with a professional for a pluck and wax every two weeks.

Paint your nails with sensible colors or pink and whites. There is only one excuse for ugly, torn or slightly dirty nails. If, and only if, you are speaking with the Landscape Association, at the Union Hall or to blue-collar men and women, and they have already endorsed you.

As you shake hands—make the laudable excuse, "Excuse my hands, this weekend I was pulling weeds, changing the oil in my 57 Chevy and helping my husband build a tree house for the children,' roll your eyes, and say with an audible sigh, 'does anyone have advice on what to use to get my hands clean? I have to meet with the Chamber of Commerce tomorrow."

Granted, you are what you wear. But, ultimately, your posture will decide how you are perceived. Hold that tummy in, firmly plant your weight evenly on both feet. Bend your knees slightly or you'll faint. Practice standing comfortably, in front of a full-length mirror. Move with elegance—from your hip joint, not from your knees.

Watch Your Weight and Eat Healthy

DO

★ Wear a single-colored dress with the hem just above or just below the knee.

★ Wear a jacket or sweater jacket with dresses or skirts.

★ Pantsuits must be the same color, top and bottom, and fit perfectly.

★ Make sure shoes are professional: closed toe and with a heel no higher than 3 inches.

★ Wear blouses of blue, white or cream—do not wear prints or stripes on a TV interview.

★ Always keep a jewel colored or robin egg blue jacket or blouse for your TV interview in the designated campaign car.

★ Always have your cotton blouses washed and starched by a professional dry cleaner.

★ Use deodorant and powder with a light scent.

★ Always wear a clean wedding ring or band if you are married or widowed.

★ Match the metal on your rings with your watch.

★ Wear as impressive a watch as you can afford. A sturdy look is more impressive than something dainty. Solid looking watches include Tag, Rolex or Omega.

★ Make sure all warts, bumps and gross looking things on your face, neck and hands have been removed by a dermatologist.

★ Use your jacket pocket for mints, keys and business cards.

★ Carry your car key, $10 in one-dollar bills, lipstick, business cards, a pen and mints in your pocket or a tiny kit hidden under your arm, inside your bra.

★ Always carry breath mints; loose in your pocket is better than the too bulky or the obvious Tic-Tac case.

★ Carry ten one dollar bills for tips and to buy your first (and only) glass of wine (diluted, ¼ wine and ¾ soda or water) at no-host evening functions.

★ Only wear jeans if you also wear a large belt buckle and a jacket.

★ When you attend a local sporting event, wear khakis and a shirt with a collar. If you must wear a t-shirt with a logo, wear it over the top of your blouse with the collar of your blouse showing. A sleeveless blouse is the least bulky under a long sleeved sweatshirt.

DO NOT EVER

★ Chew gum.

★ Wear large drop earrings and bangles that clink at the wrist.

★ Ever wear a mini skirt *or* skirts to the ankles.

★ Ever wear a white blouse, checks or stripes for a TV interview.

★ Carry a handbag.

★ Wear a swimsuit or swimsuit with a cover up in public. Even if you campaign at a swimming party, do not wear anything other than a starched cotton shirt and a skirt/pants with sensible shoes, or a simple dress *with sleeves.* No muumuus, ever!

★ Wear shorts, Bermuda shorts, skorts or tights that act as pants.

★ Wear a sleeveless blouse or a tight button-up blouse that might splay open.

★ Wear a deep cut scoop or deep v-neck top with over ½ of your breasts showing.

★ Never wear holey jeans, a t-shirt, sweats or a sweatshirt in public.

★ Or, wear tennis shoes, sandals, open-toe/heel shoes, flip flops or spike heels.

★ Carry a large purse.

★ Wear a watch with a plastic band.

★ Spray loads of perfume on your body or clothes.

Practice sitting tall in your candidate costumes and while sitting tall, if you cross your legs, cross them at the knee, that means both knees are flush and a little toe is touching the ankle. On the dais, it is often better to simply cross the ankles with your knees held together, legs swept to the side. Be sure to nonchalantly inspect the tablecloth on the head table—you may get all comfy with a wide stance and later find out you were caught being inappropriate. "OMG! Are you telling me the tablecloth wasn't draped all the way to the floor?"

Hold in your stomach, raise your chin just slightly, and practice walking into a room. People must notice that you have arrived.

Shoulders back, head high, smiling eyes, slowly peruse the room. Move your head up in an almost imperceptible chin thrust. This motion is the political convincing, *Whatsup* signal.

For the shy person, these five seconds of standing erect and confident will seem to be an eternity. The purpose to mouth a fake "Hi" and the ever so slight Whatsup chin thrust is to cause people at the party or in the audience think, Geese, she knows a lot of people here, I'd like to meet her.

Another reason you pause erect, professional and confident at the entrance of any venue is to get control of your pounding heart, rushing adrenaline and to figure out where the bar might be. Everyone will watch your every move, so you had better practice the look and actions of a candidate. You want your voters to point you out to people not yet sold on you, and say with pride and confidence; "She's got my vote."

PART TWO

GET SET!

★ ★ ★

"The whole game is chemistry.
It's what the voter gets in his gut."

Ed Rollins, In Maureen Dowd, "Finding Mr. Right:
In elections as in Romance, It's often a matter of chemistry."
New York Times, 8 March 1992

★ **Are You Ready?**

★ **Political Jargon**

★ **Campaign Kits**

★ **Branding: Signs, Business Cards and Media**

★ **File for Office**

★ **The Campaign Office**

★ **Find the Voters**

THE PURPOSE OF **Part 2, Get Ready!** is to remind you about political jargon, how branding techniques will make you stand out, how and when to file for office, how much money you'll need from now up to the Primary, how to ask for campaign contributions and finally, how to organize a basic political strategy by utilizing the campaign office, voter rolls, maps and a three month calendar.

Mark Hannah, the Republican kingmaker of the late 20th century, told a group of would-be candidates about priorities: "The first thing is money, and I can't remember what the second one is." We also believe that cash is king, and so, what is the queen? It's a three-way tie between how you look, and what you say, and how you say it.

You know who you are and why you are running for office. You have reasoned out a secretive rationale for seeking public office. It took you just a few days to evaluate the negatives, you have written and practiced short and longer versions of the vision speech and you know what to say when anyone asks, "why are you running?"

Plenty of time has been invested in exploring the pros and cons of local issues, you have talked and listened to the Titans involved with those issues and know precisely who will benefit politically or financially by every controversial and ho hum local issue.

You are clear on the hot issues of the community and you have selected three to six that appear to be significant to both the voters and Titans. In addition, you are able to discuss the pros and cons of many other issues in an agreeable or forceful way.

The focus now is on the next three or four months out from the primary. Let's assume that the primary election is in June and the general is in November. It is now March or April, there is a three-month window until the Primary election.

Our assumption is you already know the political process and have learned the terminology and idiomatic usage by following local issues. We take for granted you have studied both state and local current affairs; local political jargon often mirrors state and regional current controversy. If you are not confident, start reading the opinion pages of local and national newspapers and watch both FOX and MSNBC.

Make sure you are taking home delivery of the local newspaper. Next, go to the library, Internet or a bookstore and peruse the late *New York Times* Pulitzer Prize winning columnist, William Safires' 1968 *Dictionary of Political Jargon*. Look for the fifth edition. Safire gives almost all the jargon and political slang you will need to appear professional and in the know.

The Use of bureaucratic verbiages like fuzzy math, game plan, linkage, silent majority, cover-up, deep-six, dirty tricks, stonewalling, depth polling, nattering nabobs of negativism, policy wonk, scorched earth, and thought police, plus phrases like Reagan's "evil empire," George W. Bush's "axis of evil," and Bill Clinton's "what the meaning of 'is' is" are all included.

If you intend to keep up with incumbent candidates, you must memorize and identify every name, nickname and acronym used in your municipality, and be familiar with most of the city, state and federal laws that might be used in conversation. This little bit of knowledge will make you likeable and trustworthy, to both the Titans and political junkies.

You may look good and speak well; but it's what's happening behind the scenes that makes a winning ruthless and calculating campaign. These last few items are easy to assemble and you will thank me over and over.

1. Assemble the campaign car kit,
2. the refresher kit,
3. the media package and
4. the campaign headquarters.

Branding Made Simple

GOOD GRIEF, HOW silly is that? I have to be an expert on the cosmos of my district and now I have to decide which typeset and colors to use for my signs and brochures? The font and color scheme selected for branding your public campaign is serious business. I agree, branding is probably best left up to the professionals. However, I assume, you do not have a campaign consultant running your campaign: it's just you and me, so let's get started.

Before deciding on the location of your campaign office and before you file your intent to run, you will have already selected a signature typeset (font), slogan, logo and a two-color scheme to use on business cards, yard signs and nametags.

Your slogan, symbol, song and logo are a personal choice, and not imperative, so I won't delve too much into those decisions. That said, it never hurts to pick an image or slogan unique to your town: like the mountains, a river, a train, whatever you know will cause voters to feel nostalgic about where they live. Happily, voters will connect your name with what they love about the community— and that warm fuzzy feeling may translate into both calculated and out of the blue votes.

A campaign song is whatever gets your heart racing. If you officially use more than a few bars, you'll have to ask for permission and/or pay royalties. Frank Sinatra's, *My Town* or *My Way,* John Mellencamp's *Small Town*, Bruce Springsteen's *Born in the USA,* John Hall's *Still the One* would work well. I don't know if I would use Bobby McFerrin's *Don't Worry be Happy*—but for sure I'd crank up Tom Petty's *I won't Back down.*

The key to ballot name recognition is to connect with the voters through visual repetition. The name of the branding game is solely for name recognition. If you decide on a symbol, logo and slogan, it must always be printed in the same typeset, be the exact same color and designed with the slogan or logo in exactly the same location—on every piece of campaign literature. Everything with your name must be consistent, distinct, and easily read—even from a distance.

Sign lettering should always be large and easy to read. Don't agonize over a font: script and fancy lettering does not say anything about you except, I have no idea what I am doing. I suggest any block style typeset similar to Arial Bold Block. Go ahead and pick Arial Bold Block or one of it's cousins and move on to a color scheme.

Campaign colors matter. A color scheme has a purpose, similar to the selection of your candidate uniform and the way you address an audience—color is all about defining you. You owe the Titans and the voters when you dress and speak well and you owe those driving around to notice your signs and say to themselves—she's running a smooth and professional campaign.

To blast your name recognition in a simple but pleasing format and to keep printing costs to a minimum, I suggest a one-color scheme. The more colors you have on your signs or brochures, the more it costs. The good news is whatever base color you print on, is actually the second color. If you chose, white paper or poster board as the base, then whatever color you select for the lettering, will be the secondary color.

If you decide on a white base with colored letters—then put a two-inch frame around the edges of the sign in the letter color—and conversely—if you have white words, then put a white edge. Here are color options I have seen and know work perfectly:

★ Dark purple base with white letters or white base with dark purple letters
★ Forest green base with white letters or white base with green letters
★ Deep dark blue base (not navy) and white letters or white base with blue letters

Pastels, black and white and anything neon are usually poor combinations. Red, white, and blue has seen its better days too. That's not to say those color schemes are taboo—it depends on your community and which office you are seeking and who your constituents are.

School board candidates often pick school bus yellow with black lettering. Water district candidates may use blue and white to remind folks of cool clean water. Some may select a forest green background with white lettering just because it is clean and easy to read.

Just last week I noticed a hot pink with white words lined in black (that's three colors since the base color of the sign is white), granted the hot pink was a bit ultra feminine but the candidates name was Bette—so the hot pink sign works for her. I remembered her name and that's just what you want the voters to get from your signs: ballot name recognition.

NAMETAGS AND BUSINESS CARDS. Always use the same color combinations on nametags and business cards—as on the yard and arterial (roadside) signs. Nametags and business cards are simple to order over the Internet or through a local print shop. There is a lead-time of about five to ten days for both business cards and nametags, so think ahead.

Business cards usually have your picture and ballot name on the front side and a list of your qualifications, website and phone number on the flipside. Both nametags and business cards reinforce your ballot name and the office you are seeking—printed, of course, in the same font as your signs.

The base color of the nametag is the dominant campaign color. Most big box office supply stores will help with the design. It should be about 4" x 3". Your ballot name is on the top line, as large as possible and the position you are seeking, in smaller letters, under your name.

Some great discussions will arise if you put the word' for' in tiny, but readable cursive font, on the line between your name and the office you are seeking. Your opponents may complain that the nametag reads as if you are the incumbent.

If accused of this, act shocked and have a kind, but perplexed look on your face: somewhere in between—a sweet version of, *"Are you nuts?"* and *"I will be the incumbent... someday."* All the same, for sure, there will be some news coverage and that is good positive exposure.

Always wear your nametag about six inches below your left shoulder. In that position, when you shake hands, people just naturally look at your lapel pin. Of course, do not pin the nametag on your bosom.

If your last name (family name/surname) is long or difficult to pronounce or to identify (on the primary ballot), use your first name instead. If both your first name and your last name are difficult to pronounce: you are in trouble. However, if you register a ballot name with a nickname (as a middle name) you may be able to successfully use the nickname in large print and the unpronounceable surname as small print—and still be recognizable on the ballot. For example: Samuel 'nomorewar' Stephens, Nancy 'Occupy' Price or Rahphel 'Ralph' Ozegingeria. That said, kooky middle named candidates, usually do not win the primary.

YARD AND ARTERIAL SIGNS. Selecting a company to manufacture nametag, yard signs and brochures is just an Internet click away. I like www.victorystore.com for professional creative ideas. Victory Store offers personalized service for imprinted items like door hangers, pink ribbon items (breast cancer advocacy items-remember the hot pink sign), fans, banners, bumper stickers, magnets, stickers, yard signs, key rings, pens and sundry items like the best ever giveaway: a fingernail file in red white and blue with my ballot name in bold letters. Also wildly popular is the seven-day pillbox, imprinted with your ballot name on top.

Another website is www.runandwin.com. Please, don't be a chump and pay for online design assistance. Online political websites might ask for a set up fee, but they will never ask you to pay for design assistance. Consider ordering yard signs from the Internet companies.

That said, it may be cheaper to use a local sign shop for larger freeway and arterial road signs. Using a local sign shop assures you 'buy local' and eliminates shipping costs. Often there is only one or two cheap sign shops in town—you may be able to see what the opposition is doing with their signage when you pick up your signs.

Most yard signs (real estate 'for sale' size) and arterial road signs (4' x 6') are attached to rebar poles pounded into the ground with brute strength and a rebar pounder. Ask contractor Titans to donate rebar as an in-kind gift or purchase the poles at a big box building supply. (Always record in-kind donations on the expense report). The short 3-foot rebar is for smaller yard signs and the 5-foot is for the larger arterial signs. Clustered into groups of 10, they are heavy. Always use gloves when handling rebar, they are dirty.

To pound the rebar into the ground, first eyeball the ideal traffic vantage points, next pound two rebar poles about 4.5 feet apart. Then, with an ice pick, poke a hole in all four corners of the sign; thread a clear plastic ten-inch cable tie through the ice pick holes. Attach the four corners securely with the cable ties onto the rebar. I guarantee, neither wind nor rain will move that sign. If your signs are uber secure—you won't have to go back after a big storm to find them looking forlorn and beaten. Fallen signs appear sloppy and reflect poorly on the campaign. Secure yard signs the same way—except with the shorter rebar stakes.

Your name should be seen everywhere in town. It's a sign war, and you are the General in charge of selecting the streets, avenues, tree limbs, front yards and freeway entrances to broadcast your ballot name.

You are in charge, unless of course, you have wooed those three to five dedicated women, if so, they will be out pounding rebar and finding yards to post your signs. That includes both alternate short-cut corners and major arterial roads. You attach signs to posts, where a signs says 'post no bills or signs,' on property that says 'no trespassing' and as often as possible, next to or near opponents' signs.

Never touch your opponents' signs, or post anything over them. Nearby is ok and, if you feel the need, you might position your sign 5-10 feet in front of your opponents'

It is forbidden to attach political signs to private fences, causeway, thruway and freeway entrances. However, I say, go ahead and attach signs to the major on and off ramps chain link fences—those signs may or may not be removed. The removed signs are usually easy to retrieve and you are not going to jail. The private fence owners will either leave it or destroy it. Lost or destroyed signs are the cost of doing campaign business.

Record, in a small notebook, labeled YARD SIGNS, where you locate your signs. Keep the yard sign notebook in the designated campaign car and ask anyone who pounds a large sign or yard sign to text you the name and address. You are the responsible party to send a thank you note. Don't miss the opportunity to be seen hanging signs and pounding rebar in and on the major arterial roadside fences and fields on both Saturday and Sunday afternoons. You are in church on Sunday mornings.

Signs, brochures, nametags, giveaways, and business cards are useless unless they are seen everywhere. To be at the top of voters' minds, run radio ads and post signs in repetition; a seeming echo blast of your 15-second radio ads should be streaming the neighborhood airwaves, and all vacant lots must be littered with your stalwart signs blasting your ballot name. Your ballot name is everywhere—don't stop littering the vacant lots, fences, yards and air waves—even if you overhear a relative or friend say, "If I hear that radio ad one more time am going to puke."

A week before the primary election, there must not be any printed material left in the backseat, trunk, garage, dining room table, stacked at the local library or in partisan political offices. Attach multiple printed cards, brochures or yard signs with stick glue or a stapler onto poster board or thin 3x5 plywood pieces and find good use for them. I like to think of these left over multiple placements of brochures, business cards and signs as pre-primary cluster bombs. Plaster those clustered posters everywhere.

Place them near polling places and early voting venues (within the acceptable areas and/or a certain number of feet from the entrance of the polls—check your laws). You want voters to have your ballot name be the last thing they see before they go into the polls to vote.

If you end up not getting into the general election, a quick way to get your signs off yards and arterials is to offer 25 cents for every yard sign and $1.00 for every big sign returned to your campaign headquarters backyard.

An article in the local newspaper, with a picture of a Boy Scout pulling up your signs, could be just the positive press you need to relieve the funk of losing. And funk it will be, the phone stops ringing and the only invitation you'll receive will be to attend a 'thank you' party for the person that beat you.

SLOGANS or mottos; sometimes backfire. But, if you must, base a slogan loosely on your vision statement and the three dominate vision issues. Granted, it is professional to use a slogan or a motto and a candidate without one or the other is out of the ordinary. However, it's my position that ultimately the ballot name is what the voter must remember on Election Day. That said, here are more than a few mottos and slogans.

- ★ A strong voice for Torrance
- ★ Jean has clear principles...and she has a record to prove it
- ★ Accountability for...education, city parks, waste pickup, conservation
- ★ Getting to the root of the problem
- ★ Common sense leadership
- ★ It's time for a change
- ★ New Leadership for Evergreen's future
- ★ Progress...without the Politics
- ★ Making Golden Meadows a better place to live
- ★ Strength and honor
- ★ Accountability through Action
- ★ Change "business as usual"
- ★ Uncompromising Values for a Secure tomorrow
- ★ Bringing People together and getting things done
- ★ Honest. Experienced. Independent.
- ★ An honest conservative with the courage to fight for us!
- ★ The courage to do what's right
- ★ Let's work together
- ★ Strong Willed and Principled
- ★ Promises Made—Promises Kept

YOUR JPEG HEADSHOT is important. It's given to print media and it's front and center on your business card. Many voters will decide to vote for you (or not) based on the photograph in the local newspaper, your business card or brochure.

A professional photographer is not imperative, but a homemade headshot out of focus or with inappropriate clothing or background is a vote loser That said, if your choice is to take a homemade photo, it must have a simple background and be in focus.

Pull your hair off your face and out of your eyes. Apply makeup all over your face—with a slight bit of lighter beige under your eyes down to the bottom of the eye orbit bone—brush the sides of your cheeks with blush and use a darker blush or an instant tan cream under your jaw and chin line. Wear sensible earrings.

A pale blue blouse photographs better than pure white. Wear a deep blue or brown suit jacket, not black. The blouse collar should be open, upright and balanced perfectly on both sides of your neck. The jacket should look well fitted at the shoulders and a string of pearls resting just below the crook of the neck finishes off the ruthless friendly candidate look. It's the old fashioned woman look, and sadly, it's the look the voters expect a woman politician to portray.

The black and white headshot is calculated. Your smile should be obvious but not toothy. The eyes need to be friendly, honest and open wide. Not in a wide eyed surprised, eyebrows up—but more: I care and love you and I'm interested in what you think. Keep your eyes straight on the voter. Always use a blank or slightly textured background.

Never keep or submit a photo of you looking down or to the side. Side glancing or eyes pointed upward and profile shots are often used by the media to a portray a sneaky, dishonest or ashamed candidate.

The black and white headshot is part of the media package, placed on the front of your business card and taped onto the bathroom mirror. Peggy knows the importance of posting a snapshot on the bathroom mirror: she teaches all progressives this bathroom mirror lesson: your hairstyle must not change one iota during the campaign season.

It's nice to also have a family picture too. This photo is informal and very friendly. Include pets. I like children to fold their arms across the chest—but only if they give a toothy grin. An outdoor shot at a local park or well-known place in town, works well to amplify the family image, include your parents too.

Campaign Kits

AFTER TAKING THE photograph and downloading it into your computer, seriously, start looking in the garage, office and kitchen junk drawer for useful stuff you will need to organize a professional campaign table.

First, buy or find a sturdy box or a small suitcase on wheels, one you can push or pull and easily lift. Make sure whatever you use fits in the backseat or in the trunk of the designated candidate car and you can lift it in and out with ease. Inside the Campaign Car Kit is everything necessary to set up a table for a pre-debate or a meet and greet.

★ Lightweight card table
★ Red checkered tablecloth
★ Business easel to mount yard sign
★ Yard signs to give away
★ Mints or M&M's with your ballot name printed
★ Printed ballot name finger nail files
★ Business cards
★ Duct and clear tape
★ Mini water bottles
★ Pens and pencils
★ Yellow lined pad to record volunteers & friends emails
★ Baskets to hold mints

You or your volunteers will set up the candidate table at meet and greets and debates. What is important is both you and the table and are approachable, folksy, competent and professional. If there is a lull with the crowd—walk around and hand out your promotional fingernail files to friends and family of the other candidates, they all vote. Always stand at the edge of the table and not behind the table—never position your table too near your opponents.

The Refresher Kit

PUT WHATEVER KEEPS you looking professional and fresh in this small but imperative kit. Including your normal face makeup sundries, I would include at a minimum: toothbrush and paste, a bottle of water, floss, breath mints, a large mirror, lipstick, brush, hairspray, makeup remover, lightly scented hand lotion and a matching scented powder. The purpose of the kit is clean yourself up between appearances. Never park near the entrance of the venue and fix yourself up. Remember the U-Tube film of Presidential hopeful John Edwards fluffing his hair with the looping Bernstein song, "*I feel pretty, Oh so pretty*" in the background?

The last campaign kit to organize is not really a kit. Nevertheless, it is important and again imperative. Pack into a tiny coin purse: breath mints, $10 in one-dollar bills, a tiny lip stain and a few business cards. The tiny emergency toiletry and tip/drink kit belongs in an inconspicuous pocket, inside your bra or wedged into your waistband. Ruthless candidates should not carry a purse; you need both hands to embrace, shake hands and float cheek kisses.

The Campaign Office

I HOPE THAT the campaign office or workspace is in your home or garage. The hitch with an office outside your home is your hair has to be perfect and you must be dressed up in a candidate uniform just to go check on anything. Lucky you, if your campaign office is at home; you may be able to stay in your robe and slippers until noon.

Oh, you have a 9 to 5 job, bad luck. If you are at work all day, set up your campaign office at home and make sure there is good light source; you'll be working all hours of the night in the office. Likely you'll be on a first name basis with the grave yard shift at the 24 hour print shop, convenience store and your favorite fast food joint.

Hearing your voice on the radio saying, "I approved this message" is sweet. Nevertheless, meet and greets and one to one introductions to the voter are significantly more important than sitting in a nice campaign office all alone.

That's why the office is bare bones and run on shoestring. Really, all you need are two blank walls, one card table, four folding chairs and two cell phones (each with different phone numbers) plus a fax, computer, printer, pens and pencils, sticky yellow notes, yellow markers, a few clip boards, a package of manila envelopes and three or four (one each for the months before the primary) stand alone monthly jumbo wall calendars.

One phone line is for voice mail only, the ringer is turned off; no one ever answers that phone (it is probably is attached to the fax). That lone mute voice mail phone is labeled, HOT LINE. The voice message, in your voice, announces to interested voters where you are speaking that week. Voters are encouraged to leave an invitation or message.

The other phone line is for making calls to contributors or political action groups; this is also your private cell phone. It would be nice to have caller identification on all phones.

THE CAMPAIGN CALENDAR is your campaign strategy. It lives and breathes within the monthly wall calendars. Enter, in pencil, every public meeting that concerns the voters in your district, formal meetings where your opponent(s) are speaking, your walk and talk schedule and every social function you can get an invite and buy an invite. Here are a few more.

★ Early voting dates
★ Last date to register to vote
★ Campaign revenue and expenditure due dates (circled in red)
★ Monthly Chamber of Commerce mixers
★ University and high school football games
★ Major holidays and parades
★ Your weekly Toastmaster meeting
★ Monthly meetings of your political party
★ Any debates that you have been invited to attend
★ All political parties' meetings
★ Men's and Women's club meetings
★ Annual social and non-profit functions: museums, libraries, musicals, run for funs, school reunions, business openings, ribbon cuttings, and everything else you can find on the Internet and in your local newspaper

As the campaign progresses, check the alternative paper and the local paper at least two to three times a week for clubs and gatherings of more than 10 people.

Getting to Know the Voters

TO BEGIN THE process of getting to know your precincts: organize or attend a meet and greet. A meet and greet is a formal or informal gathering, with more than 10 attendees who, you hope or calculate, are in your voting precincts or district. Always arrive 10 to 15 minutes early to give plenty of time to work the room—by yourself or with a handler. You also want the person in charge (a gatekeeper) to introduce you from the dais. So find the person in charge as soon as you arrive, butter him/her up and hand her your business card.

The objective is to be introduced and touch everyone; either on the shoulder, elbow or with a hand shake. Work the room, introduce yourself to everyone you see and while working the room, put at least two business cards on each table. As the meeting begins, sit down in the back of the room. If you're lucky enough to be introduced; stand up straight: and wave your hand above your head.

The purpose of positioning yourself in the back of the room is so the audience must look for you. The other reason: if you slip out early or escape to the restroom—it is not obvious you're taking a powder.

It's a waste of time to stay all the way to the end of most meetings. Ask a friend, family member or hire a driver to drop you off in front of each venue, that way the designated campaign car is waiting in front of the venue and ready to shuttle you on to the next venue. Realistically, you should schedule at least five opportunities to meet voters—every single day and/or evening of the week.

Being seen and introduced at five gatherings a day, does not exclude the mandatory three campaign contribution phone calls or the obligatory additional three in person requests for a campaign contribution—each equally as important to a winning strategy.

Occasionally you won't be invited to a function. If you are running in a non-partisan race you should be welcome at all functions—in a non-partisan way—but you are more welcome at the functions of the party you are registered. If you intend to defy being left out of an event, and you are sure most of the attendees don't despise your vision: then dress for the occasion, stand at the exit door, put on a big smile and hand out your business cards to the folks as they depart.

Those voters, who may or may not be from your precincts, are nevertheless <u>your</u> captive audience, they will look at you, your nametag and your bright cheerful smile and hear you say, *"Hi, I'm Sally, and I'm running for School Board, district 8. "I'm on your side,"* you are not exactly sure what, *'I'm on your side'* means, but neither do the people streaming into the function.

Go ahead and disregard logic and ignore cold shoulders. If a good number of folks have demonstrated that they despise your vision or you get the uh-oh gut feeling that you are unwelcome at an opposition political party function—post a lawn sign in front of the entrance. Or, be gutsy, the night before the event—put a big sign on your car and park across the street of the partisan venue.

Even though, I believe in being gutsy and aggressive when campaigning, you still must make a good impression on everyone you meet. A social get-together with predominately-opposite political party attendees is all it takes to show that wonderful side of yourself: you know the gracious and malleable side of your personality. "Well, she can't be that horrid if she's been invited here, and look there's her husband; you know he's the president of the Republican Men's club."

My printed material went out every Saturday, along with the officially endorsed candidates. Even if the union bosses had abandoned me, I remained true blue and made sure the union bug (the small symbol that shows a union shop did the printing) was on all my brochures.

On super Saturdays when the union members group and rubber band brochures together in piles; for the rank and file, to walk precincts and tout the candidates: I showed up smiling and glad handing—cookies in one hand and my brochures in the other (bless their hearts; they didn't know I wasn't union endorsed). A few bags of cookies, some chutzpah and a sincere friendliness assured my brochures and business cards landed on thousands of doorsteps and went into hundreds of pay envelopes.

Another clandestine vote getting story is from my friend, former Judge Robert Coates: he walked up and down the aisles of a San Diego Costco until a manager told him, *'Goodness we don't allow this here'*, he acted surprised and looked deeply into her eyes, *'Well, I appreciate your support; I am up for re-election.'* Coates, chagrin but flushed with the knowledge he had just met over 100 potential voters, left the store triumphant.

To get your name out there, to touch voters hearts and to make an impression; you must be a surreptitious, sly and smartly organized ruthless candidate. It's an easy maneuver to canvas the cars in a supermarket parking lot with your business cards, then go inside to do some grocery shopping, all dressed in your precinct walking candidate uniform and don't forget to give a doe eyed smile of love for everyone you pass in aisle.

Show your true grit every time you try any of our techniques. Some candidates bring their children or small pets with them to supermarkets and when walking the precinct. Why? Because women voters are more likely to open the door or enter into a conversation with a candidate sporting a child or a loveable small dog.

Walk tall, smile without showing your teeth and make your eyes shine with love for everyone you greet. If there is a sign on the door that says no solicitors, that means you. If you are told repeatedly, "Goodness, we don't allow this here," you are doing your job as a candidate. Be courteous and make your exit gracefully. Keep in mind Judge Bob Coates Costco secret weapon—a smile and a genuine apology for not knowing the Costco rules. Not only did he make contact with multitudes of voters but he also made a positive impression on the store manager.

Every couple of weeks the ruthless candidate should take an inventory of where the campaign is succeeding and where it is not.

Do not get depressed—if 8 weeks out from the primary, you get a sinking feeling that you've made a mistake and you want to quit.

There will be times of discouragement, if this were easy, everyone would be doing it.

File for Office

TUCK THE AGONY of defeat and the euphoria of winning into the recesses of your mind—it's time to file for office. I like a Friday afternoon because unless it is the first day or the last day to file, reporters will not be waiting at the registrar of voters (or wherever you file). Bring something that proves your permanent address, like an electric or water bill and at least two picture ID's and a personal check and an entourage.

The moment you sign your name on the filing papers and pay the filing fee: you must in thought, word, deed and candidate uniform—personify a cunning and ruthless candidate. When you neatly sign your name on the official paperwork, you will have already spent at least $1,000. Secured to your vibrant blue jacket is a magnetic backed nametag and in your pocket, at least 10 business cards.

You have 490 more professional two-color business cards in a long slim box out in the designated campaign car and two extra nametags in the glove compartment, the campaign car kit, the refresher kit and the tiny cosmetic kit are all tidily stacked in the back seat too.

At least twenty lawn size signs, two large road signs, and one large cloth sign to drape over the side of your car (or to attach as a drape on a 4 x 8 table) are piled up against the walls in the campaign office.

After you have paid the fee and filed the official paperwork, it's time to open a campaign contribution checking account. Go to a local bank or savings and loan armed with: the second $1,000 (you found in your savings or from a cash advance from a credit card). Bring official stamped paperwork that proves you have filed to run, plus two picture ID's and again, something that proves where you live—like an electric, water or property tax bill.

Order plain checks with duplicate thermal carbon paper. Instead of your name—make up a campaign title. Something like: FRIENDS OF <u>YOUR BALLOT NAME</u>. Under the campaign title, place the official PO Box number (not your home address) and finally use the campaign office voicemail phone number (the fax number). If you have a slogan you could add that under the telephone number.

It is smart to identify and to designate an additional person authorized to write or deposit checks. Of course, that means the person designated as your 'second' comes along to the bank and need we mention, is trustworthy, has never bounced a check and has no felony charges pending.

The First Media Interview

IF YOU FILE on Friday afternoon, local print media may not realize you have filed until Monday morning. If a daily print journalist phones on Friday, she will file her article for the Saturday edition or if she calls on Monday, she will be writing an article for the Tuesday edition.

Here is when the basic media package comes in handy. Ask if she would like a media package emailed to her while you are chatting. Just that little act will impress the journalist—which may translate into a better well thought out article about you.

What's included in the media package? Traditionally, it has three pages; a candidate resume (with your vision statement), a black and white jpeg headshot and a cover sheet with your phone number, PO Box and website.

But, what if it's not just the print media but also the TV/radio journalist media person who calls, he may need copy for the Friday 6 o'clock news and he just may need to fill some time. He will ask to send out a film crew or interview you right over the phone. Either way, say yes.

Yikes, the film crew is on its way. First, take a couple of Tylenol or if you are lucky, you'll find a half of a Xanax in the medicine cabinet; either one will calm the nerves. A shot of whiskey may show up on your breath so keep it hidden in the pantry; toss it down after the interview.

Look in the mirror, how do you look? Make sure your hair and makeup is just right. Do not put on extra makeup. Do not emphasize the cheeks or darken around the eyes. Well, maybe some under eye lightly tinted cream might be ok—I am sure you didn't get much sleep last night.

The key to a good interview is to give the camera operator or journalist a simple and sincere three to five second sound clip. It's a head and shoulder shot with a question from the journalist and two-sentence reply from you—that's it. You have seen this routine interview a million times—you've heard it just as many times via the radio.

Make this interview count—have a blue sheet of paper folded in half (hot dog bun fold), with your ballot name printed on the side facing the journalist. The folded side facing you has one to three sentences of your vision statement or your slogan.

Smile—and do not show your teeth. You will have practiced this vision speech over and over and even so; I bet you still have to glance down at the blue cheat sheet. Don't write anything on your hands—remember what happened to former Governor Palin.

The journalist will sometimes make your candidacy a late

breaking story. You have no control over her. She will be friendly or aggressive. It shouldn't matter to you—because you are just going to stand quietly, with the doe eyed look and wait for the questions. You aren't a big talker or a big shot; you are calm and in charge.

Make every moment count. Try not to let the journalist position the sun in your eyes—turn your left shoulder to her right shoulder or vice versa. Again, don't say a word until it is necessary. Casually lick your lips and to get some saliva working. Hopefully, you tucked a mint up between your cheek and back molars when the door bell rang.

Assume the camera is running and the microphone is hot. (Look for the red dot on the front of the camera to see if the camera is on.) The camera operator will wire you with a little black round thing, threaded up under your jacket. Speak in a natural voice, don't worry the audio will be picked up.

If the journalist has a hand held microphone, you will fare just as well. No matter which microphone style is used, check your lapels and shirt collars to assure they are balanced, pat down your hair, run your tongue over your teeth to make sure there is no lipstick stuck to the front teeth and never lean into the handheld micro-phone. If you didn't before, pop the small mint into your mouth now—you don't want to dry up half way through this début.

Take your time—if you make a mistake, stop talking. Ask for a retake. Sometimes the journalist will do a retake and sometimes not. When the interview is finished—you will see the camera op-erator pack up. Hand your media package to the reporter, smile and exit gracefully. You will be a nervous wreck and probably not remember a single word said. You do not need to wave goodbye to these two. Escape into the sanctity of your home or car and try to breathe naturally.

Everything is the same for a radio interview—including clearing your throat way before you speak, licking your lips and popping a mint to gather saliva. No obviously nervous guttural phlegm voices allowed.

I promise you, all journalists will ask about a vision statement. I suspect you will be nervous and forgetful. Be ready for whatever comes, have your vision statement next to the phone and on the blue folded cheat sheet just in case.

Media Lists

THE MEDIA IS not your friend, **but** being friendly and respectful of their power is certainly in the ruthless candidate's best interest. For that reason, you must create a list of local media personalities of television, radio, local newspaper, alternative weekly papers and newsletter fame. Under each media personality name list his/her producer or editor's name, along with the phone and fax number, plus an email.

Your best sources for local television, radio and print media telephone numbers are the yellow pages of a local telephone book or better yet, the Internet. To save time, make friends with a secretary at the teacher's union or a person in a public relations company: pleadingly ask for a copy of their well-used marked-up local media information. They will probably let you borrow their dirty out-of-date copy.

Double-check every name and all telephone numbers on the laboriously self-created or gift media list. The turnover of print and media reporters is remarkable. Fax and emails numbers change often too.

If you are making your own media buys, list the deadlines for submitting your ad or press release. Additionally, you may want to include the advertising costs. Post the media list on the wall in the campaign office—above the fax machine and keep a copy in the glove compartment of your car.

When you drop off the updated and the clean media list to the friend that lent it to you, do so with panache. Insert the hard copy list in a nice new three-hole binder; include an additional copy on a thumb drive. Of course, inside the front cover put your business card and a thank you note.

I think the ruthless candidate isn't capable of being all things. That is why, if you are going to advertise—outsourcing is best. I also believe you should not spend precious time working on a Web site, rather outsource that chore too. Hire a freelance person to buy spots in the appropriate time slots and to update the Web site.

Outsourced media companies are paid a commission by the radio or TV station—about 10-15% of the total buy. If you do make your own buys—media companies (TV, radio, and print) have writers and art departments that will assist you.

Whatever the price for a good clean Web site, pay it. And while you are hiring a Web designer decide on your domain site name. For $10 you can get a domain name from a web registrar like GoDaddy.

Remember, in our online communication age: your virtual presence can mean the difference between winning and losing. Put your focus on content, online video, and blogging platforms. Social media is your friend. A Web presence is imperative to your credibility with most voters. However, if your are not savvy, don't try everything all at once.

Prioritize: a Website is imperative, Twitter is fundamental, a Facebook page essential, and then after that you can decide if having a blog site is necessary. I think it may be a great avenue, however, the downside of befriending voters on the web is that everything is in print and it can all be used against you. For more ideas try: www.blogger.com, www.wordpress.org and www.technorati.com.

GoDaddy is great for mischievous negative campaigning. A new domain, has been described as soiling one's pants: and is prefaced with the word 'spreading', then you add an opponent's last name.com. For example: www.spreadingDamonte.com

Most media people need an alert to where you will be speaking and debating. Even if you outsource media buys, the media will look forward and be expecting press releases. Think about it, if a journalist isn't aware of where you are or what you are saying: how will you get some ink?

How to Write a Basic Press Release

IT'S EASY TO write a press release. Use your homemade letterhead, be sure to put the date, a contact person's telephone number: plus the lead and crucial information (who, what, where, why) in the first three or four sentences. Give just the facts in the double spaced media alert.

Details may be moot, because after reading the first few lines, a press release is often tossed. On the line, directly after the last line of the text, put the following: -00000- which means "that's all." The dash and the zeros will probably mean nada to a young journalist, but it will represent attention to detail and professionalism to the informed.

Remember, the media loves e-mail and press releases to arrive before morning assignments. Say before 9am, before the morning assignments are made, that way you alert the journalists and assignment editors what you are doing or saying.

Campaign Contributions

ARE YOU SCRATCHING your perfect-coifed head and saying to yourself, it is nice to be well heeled and buy a St John outfit, a pair of Justin cowboy boots, rent a campaign office downtown or hire a PR firm to do all the printing and media buys.

But, I'm not rich... Sure, I might be by the time I get out of office...hmmm... I hope you bit your tongue on that one. Remember, the secret mantra rationale for running is never said aloud.

Money corrupts us, as most of us know from watching the cable channels, reading weekly business magazines and tell all books; and money is what ultimately propels us to victory. The smart money defines the political winner as the candidate who solicits and reports the most contributions.

I maintain to be a ruthless candidate means to be strident, cynical and greedily gather cash from wherever you can find it. That means you get money from the 1% and appeal to the 99%. Then, you do your best to show the 99% that you could care less about the 1%.

Running for office isn't free or cheap. Shoestring campaigns do work, but not if you are running against an incumbent. That's why immediately find access to $10,000, and if that money is from friends, family or yourself, then make sure it's listed on your campaign contribution report as a loan to the campaign—similar to the loans you listed for the candidate uniform purchases. That way, you can repay both yourself and family members.

I want you to spend every penny of the $10,000 to win the primary. If there is any money left over in the campaign war chest without winning or coming in second in the primary, you will have thrown money down a rat hole. When you commit to a run for a down ticket office, you commit to win. Don't you dare have money left over and then wistfully say, "If I just would have invested in one more media buy or bought 5,000 more door hangers—I could have won."

If you are hell bent and serious, apply for at least two credit cards, each with a minimum of $10,000, and/or take out a home equity loan. Look at how much you can spare in savings accounts and calculate how much you have left on current credit card balances. The $20,000 is the total monies to be on hand for both the primary and general.

If there is any money left in your campaign account after the campaign ends—especially if you win, then naturally you will hold the ridiculously suspicious, but routine Thank You party. A Thank you party is an event held in your name, after an election, specifically to gather more campaign contributions. I have gone to Thank You parties where caterers put out great food and drink and only a handful of people attended. Days later, I read in the local newspaper; the party raised over $10,000.

The purpose of the Thank You party is to give the Titans a second chance to support your candidacy. Right now don't rely on a Thank You party, stick to raising money via the old fashioned way: dialing for dollars and appearing, in every way, a professional campaigner.

Finding the money tree is simple—target the names and companies listed on the campaign reports of the incumbent and/or previous people who ran for your office.

After you have deposited your own money into the campaign checking account, you then, ask, plead, or beg for money from friends, family and parents. Since you are the chief fundraiser, first practice on the people you know. Begin by asking for $100. And remember, you want a check, not cash, and no pledges unless you have been given the Visa card number and the expiration date. Better yet, teach family and friends to use the website Pay Pal account for a three-month pledge.

It's imperative to secure base donors. Base donors are very similar to base voters. Base simply means the voters or donors who are unwavering in their commitment to your campaign. Encourage the base donors to use Pay Pal or Stripe to donate $25 to $50 a month until the primary election.

I bet you would like me to give you the tried and true step-by-step way to raise money for the campaign. I wish I knew what worked best. When asking for money, it's like this: you suck it up and you ask. And, if they don't pony up with some money, ask for in-kind help.

Bottom line is: dialing for dollars is the tried and true, albeit old-fashioned, way to raise money for the campaign. That said, if you win the primary vote by 10%, you won't have to beg for money from anyone. A cordial telephone call will be all it takes to get a whole lot of checks in the mail.

The most difficult part of dialing for dollars will be to get past the Titan's gatekeeper (receptionist or secretary). First, introduce yourself to the gatekeeper and remind him/her of the office you are seeking. If you are lucky enough to get past this gatekeeper and talk to the Titan, start over.

Introduce yourself and the position you are seeking, make your three to five-sentence vision speech even shorter and sweeter. Then say to the Titan, "I would like you to support my campaign," stop talking. The answer will be yes, no, or maybe.

If a potential contributor seems friendly, but reluctant to give you a check, ask for and an 'in-kind' contribution by using an open-ended question. An open-ended query is one that isn't easily answered with a yes or no.

★ *"I understand times are tough right now. I have fifty color bro-chures to print; how's that your color copier of yours doing these days?"*

★ *"Your company has a standing advertising contract with the newspaper; this Sunday's paper is featuring my neighborhood, it'd be great to have a quarter page advertisement."*

★ *"I'd like to have a fund raiser next month—I sure would like to use your restaurant meeting room and I'd pay happy hour drink prices for about 50 people."*

Call businesses Monday through Friday in the morning, and homes on Sunday and Thursday evenings, and Saturday mornings after 10AM. Never solicit to a voice mail or a secretary. That said, ask everyone else for a contribution. Be persistent: it is OK to be coy but not to be shy. It is the candidate's job to smile and dial.

Dialing for dollars is an obligation of the candidate. Everyone is expecting your phone call. Most often, you will be dependent on the campaign contribution lists of previous candidates. That said, a personal visit to the big Titans trumps a phone call any day.

Note: If the check is over $100 you must pick it up yourself—the bagman cannot do the deed.

DIALING FOR DOLLARS—BUNDLERS—SAMPLE SNAIL MAIL REQUESTS While asking for contributions, you may have a couple of eye-opening incidents. A quid pro quo of cash for services is usually against the law. Randy Cohen, the New York Times ethicist columnist, wrote that, to some, giving money to a non-partisan candidate feels like a bribe, but to others it is perfectly normal. I agree with Cohen, when you ask for money from a Titan and when the check arrives it both looks and feels like a bribe, but it is normal operating procedure.

One option for the candidate, who cringes at the idea of asking for money face to face, is to send snail mail brochures to potential contributors; attached to the brochure a begging for money letter with a return envelope.

Go ahead and wimp out—send the letter. You will still have to make the phone calls; seldom will a Titan send you money without a meeting. Remember, the Titans need to make it clear to you what he/she expects from the contribution.

Here are a few begging for money snail mail letters that can be modified for your race.

★ **FROM FORMER PRESIDENT JIMMY CARTER SOLICITING FOR THE CARTER CENTER:** I believe you share something extremely important with Rosalynn and me: a deep concern for the current condition of our community and it's future in the 21st century. I encourage you to accept my invitation to support the Carter Center. Having good people like you involved will help ensure that the center remains a strong and effective organization. For your convenience, I am enclosing an envelope addressed to my attention. I look forward to hearing from you soon. With best wishes...

★ **FROM MY CAMPAIGN FOR MAYOR OF RENO, NEVADA:** They can launch anti-JD websites. They can use their limitless war chest to buy slick brochures. But, they can never stop me. It's about the hopes and lives of working families; it's about smart growth and our congested worn out roads, it's about all those costly redevelopment mistakes; and yes, it's about those secret meetings, too. You may not be able to work the precincts with me, but in a real sense, I am counting on you to be by my side.

★ **FROM THE CAMPAIGN OF JILL DERBY FOR CONGRESS RUNNING AGAINST THE (CURRENTLY APPOINTED SENATOR DEAN HELLER, R-NV) THEN A STATE OFFICE HOLDER:** Dean Heller is getting nasty. Instead of engaging in a thoughtful debate over the growing challenges we face, Dean Heller is trying to spread lies about me. I need your help to respond to Dean Heller's blatantly deceptive attack ads. I need your help right now—$25, $50, $100 or whatever you can afford...Together, we can win this race and help struggling families across the nation. We don't want to wake up on November 5th and look back on the missed opportunities in this election. Thank you for all you do.

Post three campaign contribution letters a day and follow up with a phone call four days later. Get a rhythm going: post three, call three—every day. No way—no how, will you remember who you have phoned for a contribution, who said yes, who didn't answer, who said maybe and who said call me back in a few weeks.

That's why another private notebook, to go along with the good deeds (you remember—the borderline quid pro quo booklet hidden in your lingerie drawer) and the sign locations notebook, is imperative. Include in the campaign contribution notebook: potential contributor name, telephone number, gatekeepers name, amount asked for, date check received, amount, thank you note sent, dates of 2nd thru 4th call and those dates. I'd call at least 4 times before giving up. Even then, if you see him/her at a party, brag about your momentum and ask for a contribution.

If the chicken living within you would rather sleep in a spider den than ask for money; then find, identify and locate bundlers via the social media or in the Yellow Pages. Bundlers solicit money for you from their clients and give you either one big check or many little ones. It is nice to have an honest bundler. It's not that bundlers are a bad lot, it's just that sooner or later they will ask something of you; and if you don't do what they want you will be squashed like a bug.

Candid bundlers may be difficult to find. Look for bundlers in large law, advertising and/or public relation firms. The political dog whistle for locating a probable bundler is the tout of having a former legislator or local public official on staff. Alternately, an organization may advertise an active "governmental affairs" division. Only you and other ruthless campaigners can hear the political dog whistle of a potential bundler. The astute and ruthless campaigner understands:

PR OR LAW OFFICES + GOVERNMENTAL AFFAIRS =
LOBBYIST = CONTRIBUTIONS.

Cash Contributions

HUNDRED DOLLAR BILLS, folded into an itty-bitty triangle, may be tucked in your palm during a handshake or simply folded in half and deftly put into your pocket. If someone gives cash, you are supposed to give it back, immediately. However, the lovely thing about honey-money is that if you do not give the tiny little triangle of cash back; who's to know, it just appeared and you don't know from whence it arrived.

The idea of a cash contribution is because the contributor does not want anyone to know they like you or they are afraid you might win and they need to cover their bases. Whatever the reasoning, they want to be anonymous and certainly do not want anyone to see their name listed on your campaign contribution report.

You have a decision to make. You know it is against the law to accept cash. Instead of accepting cash, the Titan or contributor may post-date a check (to be deposited after the last campaign contribution report is filed). Believe me this will not be the first time anyone has used that trick.

Using a postdated check approach will keep you off the front page of the newspaper for taking illegal cash and keep the donor off your campaign contributor lists until after you win the primary. It is up to you to check local rules and statutes to assure post-dating checks is legal.

Mr. Cohen, the guy who thinks contributions are bribes, asks us to question our scruples and to condemn campaign contributions,"...it is a quiet cry into the wind against a system that is corrupt and tainted. Bribes are dressed as campaign contributions, and it is beyond question that a big contribution buys access and influence", but you don't hear him say to not accept the money.

Swallow hard and get the campaign contributions whichever way you must. Be aggressive and sweetly or secretly accept what you are given. You have already decided if you will be honest or dishonest; it's simply a matter of how badly you want to win, and if you believe in the causes of the Titan contributors.

If you do decide to keep anonymous cash, think again. Instead write a nice cover letter about how this money order (don't deposit cash into your campaign account) was an anonymous gift and then send the money order and cover letter to your favorite charity. Attach a copy of the money order and the cover letter to your campaign expense report.

True Campaign Contribution Stories

ALL CANDIDATES HAVE campaign contributions tales. My first $500 was from a developer. He was a wonderful person, I thought. How often do you find a nice looking guy that makes you laugh? He needed a revision to a zoning law.

I agreed the zoning law needed to be amended—it made good sense for my district. Everyone else on the council agreed too, the vote was 6-0 in his favor. The evening after the vote, he feigned tiredness: after I asked him like a begging happy puppy—'come 'on, let's go get a drink.' After the vote that night, he never called or returned my calls. Sweet talking Titans are a dime a dozen. Use a lot of care when getting chummy with a Titan.

A less weepy example, but nearly as good a contribution lesson, was when I got the summons to meet some casino owners at an old dilapidated penny casino. Anyone else might have been scared witless: the father and son led me downstairs to a dark dungeon of a room. The son held the check in front of my face, I think it was $250, and said, "we expect you to vote the way we want you to vote." The father growled at the son, "never say anything like that again." I just looked at them, then at the check, and wondered if they were going to put a horse head in my bed if I didn't vote the way they wanted me to.

What the son wanted me to know—was the family was counting on me to save the penny casino from being gobbled up by eminent domain. Lucky for them, it had never made sense to me, to take one man's property to give to another man. For a freeway overpass or a new hospital wing, maybe, but to take property from one individual to give to another individual, absolutely not.

I had no problem tugging the check out of the son's hands, folding it in two, putting it into my breast pocket and telling them, I would vote any way I wanted to.

They hedged their bets and gave the same amount to my opponent—at the time, I thought that odd. It isn't unusual for contributors to pledge to both or all of the campaigns in the primary. Often contributors cannot figure out who is gathering the most momentum—until the last few weeks before the primary.

I don't remember why the father and son team gave up the casino. The building is still standing forlorn and dark. All the same, here is some of the rest of the story about the penny casino and the new owners.

As most stories go in our town of greed and intrigue, the penny casinos' next licensee and his silent partners—are now embroiled in court cases. (Although not specifically about the penny casino— eventually the penny casino license may be involved). There are claims that hundreds of millions of dollars are missing from an unrelated project; along with stories of Mafioso, money laundering and burly men demanding cash and jewelry. Ah, the stories former Pols should be telling the public.

Later in the same month of the penny casino contribution, when the momentum of my campaign was obvious to the Titans, A burly (yes, but a different one) vice president, instructed me to meet him in the Café Napa coffee shop.

We had the compulsory chitchat, it was obvious he was reluctant as he pushed a $1,000 check across the table and said to me, "If everyone is against our issue, we don't expect you to vote for us—but when everyone is voting for us, we expect you to vote for us." I ignorantly shrugged my shoulders and again greedily put the check into my breast pocket. That casino had juice. Why, even the publisher of the daily, national chain, newspaper was on its' board of directors.

Months later, after I won the primary and the general election with 60% and after figuring out what the Titans wanted me to do. I voted against the mega casino's wishes. Thereafter, there was a negative story front page under the fold, high on the back page or on the inside first page; seldom on a Saturday or buried on page 4 in the daily local Gannet newspaper, about my decisions and escapades.

It sure felt like they ganged up on me. The same publisher who was on the mega casino board of directors—also belonged to a network of Titans and while the network was gorging themselves at the public trough a thought came to some citizens to picket the newspaper in protest.

A group led by my friend, Willy, targeted the newspaper publisher and the network of greedy Titans. On a cold sunny Saturday afternoon, on the sidewalk, near the newspaper's parking entrance a line of picketers—greeted by supportive honks from passing cars.

A few days after the picketing, the publisher was kicked upstairs, to head up the entire region; her reign of terror as both as a devotee of the network and as an unofficial advocate of the downtown Titans was over. The network had nowhere to hide and it began to crumble.

In the past ten years, that same network of vicious Titans who made so many ghastly mistakes for our community still thinks they are hot stuff. There is one person, who sleeps in the downtown bed he and his network pals created, and as political karma goes, it seems he reigns as a lord of the flies.

Here's one final campaign contribution story. The privately owned casino mogul handed me a check. It was for $100. I pushed the check back to the casino owner, smiled and said to him, "I have shoes that cost more than that. I need twice as much." He laughed, tore up the check and wrote me a check for twice as much.

PART THREE

GO!

★ ★ ★

*"If I was runnin' f'r office, I'd change me name,
an' have printed on me cards:
'Give him a chanst; he can't be worse."*

Finley Peter Dunne (1867-1936)

★ HARDBALL TACTICS

★ MOMENTUM

★ JOURNALISTS AND WHISPERERS

★ MATHEMATICAL ALGORITHMS

★ SECRETS OF THE PRECINCT MAPS AND WALKING MAPS

★ USEFUL STRATEGIES

★ FAKE IT UNTIL YOU MAKE IT

★ TO DO LIST

Playing Political Hardball

PLAYING HARDBALL IS complicated. You are the new kid on the block—so you won't get much attention. There will be so much going on within the up ticket and down ticket races; that to NOT distinguish your campaign: by being outrageous, negative or unconventional, is plain dumb.

Somehow, you must make news. Even if it is mildly negative. I hope the opponents' sense your well run campaign and poke at you first. When the negativity begins, you must be ready to retaliate. When you hear or see a debilitating comment, about you or your campaign: you must respond using a counter or a guerilla attack (whisperers). Think like Mohammed Ali, float like a butterfly and sting like a bee.

Once a punch is thrown your way; you must duck and then throw one back. The candidate who refuses to use a negative campaign strategy is grossly naïve, and ignorant of the rules of political engagement. We guarantee, local print and media journalist will scoff, behind your back or to your face, at your obvious lack of negative strategy, devious behavior or retaliation.

All the opponents' supporters hate your guts. They will tell and retell stories and tales about you, stories that you swear are libelous and contemptible. You are one screwed candidate if you did not thoughtfully and thoroughly review and complete your self-assessment, make up plausible explanations for your negatives and commit those justifications or explanations to memory.

Don't waste your time or money running for office, if you don't believe in negative campaigning. Make a plan to tell the worst truths about your opponent either overtly or covertly if the need arises. That said, remember, negative campaigning is saved for retaliation. You don't have to take the first punch.

Positive Momentum

EVERY TIME YOU appear in public, have one-on-one encounters with your dry cleaner, pool boy, landscaper, and hairdresser; there will be talk. Gossip, chitchat, rumor, and conversation; every interaction the ruthless candidate encounters, is a potential defining moment of the campaign.

The goal is to surprise opponents and Titans with uncanny strategic political abilities. I believe uncanny strategic political abilities means to be silent, be nice, stay clean, don't get personal, until the day you aren't.

As soon as an opponent senses your positive momentum, they will drop a bombshell; you will feel the swoosh of an incoming, the injury, emotional pain and anguish; the likes of which you have never felt before—will blast your sensibilities, "How could they twist that episode into such a distorted lie?" you'll ask friends and volunteers in disbelief.

Easy answer, opponents must rip at your momentum: to stop yours and to boost their own. Negative isn't always about negatives either. Often an opponent will print or create a media contrast advertisement. An opponent's **contrast ad** list positive aspects about themselves and partial-half-truths about you.

That said, usually in down ticket contests, you'd be better off to use a contrast ad versus an attack ad. An **attack ad** goes after the personality or opinions of the opponent(s)—it's a stinky way of lashing out and often there's a backlash. Anyway, stick to the contrasts, in the primary, mostly because there will probably be too many opponents and not enough money for you to smear them all.

Here are a few ways to develop the contrast attack advertisement or verbal positions that show how you differ from other candidates. Try using a contrast attack with a friendly audience. The moniker sticks to your opponent(s) when the audience reacts with a laugh, a nod or a clap of approval—if so, you will have yourself a professional contrast attack.

---

* ★ Capable vs. incompetent
* ★ Conservative vs. progressive
* ★ Populist vs. elitist
* ★ Citizen vs. career Politician
* ★ Public interest vs. special interest
* ★ Reform vs. status quo
* ★ Time for a change vs. special interest
* ★ Local vs. out of touch
* ★ Visionary vs. no ideas
* ★ Independent vs. run by the lobbyists
* ★ Mainstream vs. extreme
* ★ Experienced vs. unqualified
* ★ Youthful vs. older

Fanatical Supporters

OF COURSE YOU will want supporters and volunteers—but be fore-warned they may come and go during the next few months. Just make sure that your list of supporters and volunteers are people you know and trust, but then as we said before—these are the people that may break your heart and wittingly (or not), will stab you in the back.

Treasure the dedicated and enthusiastic supporter and volunteer who may do some of your mudslinging. Work them hard and reward them with a slice of pizza a beer and a heartfelt and sincere, "Thank you." And then, after you win, appoint them to a board or commission.

In the introduction, I hinted at the deceit, backstabbing realities of the opposition. People opposed to you *will not* use reasonableness when they chat or hurl slurs about your negatives. Negatives you think are a shade of gray, are pitch black to them. With luck, your volunteers feel the same way about your opponents.

Fiendish supporters of your opponents will shout, like Representative Joe Wilson shouted out during President Obama's address to the joint session, "you lie!" or boo in unison when you are about to pivot onto an important issue and solution.

Volunteers stick together. Sometimes tanked up on wine, they will sit directly in front of you at a debate and make your life hell. The opponent supporters don't have to be nice: they are out to make the kill—so you will be stunned and forget easy answers: then in unison like a high school pep squad, they will give an audible cheer and all laugh and high five each other. During a debate, do not even look at the opponents' pep squad and don't ever attempt to win them over: they are the enemy; and they do hate you.

A sensible alternative to the barrage of the opposition shenanigans: is to be prepared. In addition to staying on message and being prepared, your volunteers could also be making hoots and hollers.

Before we tackle some defensive maneuvers let's jolt your memory: to the voter, both negatives and positives define character. Negatives are the decisions and choices that appear to the voter as bizarre or inappropriate. Unfortunately, your negatives are also decisions and choices family members have made too; like wife battery, drugs, child neglect or Sarah Palin's husband and the Alaskan secessionist club to which he allegedly belonged.

As a review: the pivot or the agreeable deflection is a defensive move away from a negative issue to a friendlier kinder issue. Here are a few more ways to make a verbal run away from negatives.

★ *Actually,…*
★ *Yes, I see your point, but let's get back to the issues.*
★ *I have heard enough about my many marriages, I'm here to discuss a solution to the…*
★ *I'm accused of being too conservative, but the bottom line is…*
★ *The fact is…*
★ *But let me tell you how it really happened…*

Thomas Bray, a columnist for the *New York Sun Newspaper* proclaimed:

"Democracy wasn't meant to be mannerly. It is an adversary process designed to filter out the worst among the contenders for public office. If the process is sometimes unappetizing, it also helps to cut down on surprises after the winner takes office."

When an opponent levels an attack at you, a response will require some previous thought. If you know yourself and remember the self-assessment exercise, you have half the body armor to shield you from the negative shotgun blast to your sensibilities. Even if I gave you some effective techniques to create a five to ten sentence reason for whatever your problems are or were—you still must be sincere and show appropriate embarrassment at being exposed.

When attacked, you pivot to your public defense. Remember, the short statements of justification, explanation, defense or an apology used as a defensive maneuver—then you swerve to the pivotal transition with an agreeable deflection. That is why I emphasize again that a written and memorized justification, explanation, defense, or apology for your negatives must be airtight and readily available from your right brain into your voice box.

The reason I put you through a grueling self-assessment was just for this; nearly anyone can say whatever they want about you and if enough people are whispering the same things, you will need to defend yourself and retaliate against your opponent. Unfortunately, until a whispered or overt charge is leveled at a casual luncheon or an attack/contrast ad runs on the local TV station or in a full page ad in the local newspaper insists you were outrageous to the police; you'll be sitting ignorant of what the public knows or doesn't know.

It's a brilliant and an amazing technique to watch how Former Speaker Newt Gingrich, by using junk yard dog tactics and an aggressive pivot against Mitt Romney, was successful, in the 2012 primary caucuses, to sway voters in South Carolina. Although Gingrich always specifically defended his negatives, it's also key to commit to memory how he pivoted: "Now, let's get back to the issues that matter..."

Again, unless you are a candidate for a Judgeship or City Attorney, don't be visible as a mean-spirited candidate. Nevertheless, the aggressor usually wins the fight. Be like Dorothy Parker, a turn of the 20th century American poet and satirist, the first thing you do in the morning is brush your teeth and sharpen your tongue. To be a credible candidate you must be calm and swift enough to nip the negatives in the bud, and when attacked even by contrasts: do as the pundits tell us: attack back and eat what you kill. Being feared is a great motivator for opponents NOT to use negative campaign techniques on you.

Sometimes a sly candidate pretends to be an underdog so they can surprise voters and Titans by exceeding expectations. Pretending to be an underdog is a nice ploy but you may tempt fate. It isn't very appealing to picture yourself as the bunny pounced on by hunting dogs. It is much like the situation when the candidate for US president, Hillary Clinton broke down in tears, looked a little pathetic and as a result people some saw her as weakened.

If you would prefer a nicer explanation of negative retaliation, then go online to Politicalstrategy.org. The site is superb with ideas and solutions to every candidate strategy query. Although, many of the ideas seem absurd, in practice they are practical. Like the idea of accusing your candidate of being desperate or un-American or by using a belly laugh as a response an opponent's message. Granted, your campaign is not a middle school girl fight, but most voters perk their ears up when they hear about a girl fight in the back parking lot.

Your odds of losing go way up if you run a clean campaign. On the other hand, tactically, negatives may work to your advantage. If you do become a victim, you have the right to fight back. That is political self-defense. In addition, sometimes appearing as an underdog allows you some leeway and a valid reason to go negative.

NEGATIVE IMPERATIVES

Here are five imperatives to keep in mind before you give the whisperer the go ahead to leak the negatives.

1. Frequently campaigns search for the silver bullet that will destroy the opponent.
2. Negative campaigns are usually a death of a thousand cuts and not quick and painless.
3. Test a negative about an opponent, if it doesn't work up an audience don't waste time on it.
4. You must keep track of statements, contributions and information that are most current.
5. Whisperers must not leak or release information without the approval of the candidate, regardless of how "damaging" the information might appear.

Now go bravely to the next section on deceptive negative branding of your opponent(s) and the art of never forgiving a slight. I propose you be a little like the character Lisbeth Salander, from Stieg Larsson's bestselling book, *The Girl with the Dragon Tattoo.* Lisbeth, is a girl who never forgave "...an affront, and made no bones about it, and to her sense of duty meant *to exact revenge for herself or her friends, was not only a right, it's an absolute duty."*

Political snickers, laughter and whispers will swirl around like little dark clouds beneath your feet all the time. To be politically aware means to notice the evil breeze as you enter a room. Every time you go to a meet and greet or a candidates' forum you'll walk through the verbal clouds. Eventually and instinctively, you will know if the clouds are dark, gray, or safe.

Whisperers and Journalists

YOU AND OPPONENTS might not blab to the face of a journalist, but whisperers will tell half-truths and innuendos to whomever else will listen, that's for sure.

The whisperer is a sneaky person who spreads nasty gossip with a smile and a shrug of the shoulders. Your whisperer says good stuff about you and bad stuff about the opponents and theirs tells bad stuff about you. Again, follow Mohammed Ali's lead and sting like a bee.

The most dedicated, indulgent and committed whisperers are often journalists, the drones who report for the local newspaper and the more slothful but perky talking heads on local TV. Well-intentioned journalists will claim they are just doing their job; in fact, they thrive on gossip, rumor and innuendo—in order to have their articles positioned at the top of the hour or front page above the fold. Seldom do they have the time to investigate and describe in detail, tainted truths or untruths.

When you filed your paperwork and paid your fee, you became a public entity, a voodoo pincushion for anyone against you or your candidacy. You can be quoted out of context and caught talking with half a sugar doughnut stuffed into your mouth, you can be photographed in your swimsuit just as you are bending over to pick up your towel, hair a mess and your stomach rolls bunched up like stacked tires at a Sears automotive showroom.

The opponent's supporters will video you on their phone cams every time they see an opportunity. Where is your whisperer? Find one as soon as possible. You don't have to be the naïve bunny in the pasture, ripped to shreds. Whisperers on both sides simply help to make an even playing field. Timing is important; and remember, you are the 'ultimate decider'. Your whisperer must *always* get your approval before releasing any nasty information.

Repeating and retelling keeps the story alive and puts just a hint of doubt in the voters mind. Never presume the public is rational, it is so easy to sway public perception. If there is a snicker from be-hind the curtain, you may be in for a surprise.

During a taped interview, a candidate for Senate in the 2010 primary midterm race, made a remark about chickens. Her point had something to do with how, in the pioneer days of the west, medical doctors accepted chickens in lieu of cash for services. From that point on, the poor woman could not get away from the clucking: both live chickens and people wearing ridiculous chicken costumes, plagued both her campaign office and appeared in meet and greet audiences and at debates. She was the favorite in the primary, but she lost.

Silly ridicules, mockery and snickers are devastating to the eager ruthless candidate. When you spin or they spin, it's shit hitting a fan. Some will get on you and some will get on your opponent. You have to decide if releasing a negative contrast or attack, thru a whisperer, will come back to haunt, stain or tarnish you—because we all know that paybacks are a bitch. Political blowback is even worse: the other side must retaliate.

A reality is that you will be judged on how you take a political negative punch. Negative campaigning, both the getting and the giving, is not just the sport of American politics; it is a test of your ability, to be stalwart and to show neither fear nor hesitation.

Tactically, poor press, may work to your advantage. If you do become a victim, you have the right to fight back. That is also self-defense. The push pull is a dandy way to make a statement about an opponent by musing: "What if you knew...."

Sometime during the campaign, you will hear a push pull statement; typically, a push pull is used in the final moments of a telephone survey. Push pull is the technique of asking a question, which is somewhat true or a half-truth to try to get a voter to see a candidate in a different light, usually in an unfavorably way.

Here are some classic push pull questions: "What if you knew...

★ the Mayor/City Manager moved into a big new house built by the same guys that got that huge non-bid city contract?

★ he married his daughters best friend?'

★ the commissioner made that vote on ethics if she didn't have something to hide in her campaign contributions?"

★ she had never seen her *not* drunk?

★ her husband worked at a strip club?

★ she had backed abortion issues last year, would you think less of her?

★ he had to recuse himself when the Tahoe Pyramid Link was discussed?

★ if he represented or owned a portion of a nearby planned housing project?

- ★ his wife got the contract for all the drapes in the hotel
- ★ he bought up that property next to the airport?
- ★ there is even a wine cellar?
- ★ she dating that old guy even though she's married?
- ★ the fatso TV reporter had bedded many of the Police?
- ★ she showed a dead fetus in her TV commercial?

No one likes a bitchy candidate that is hard-edged, scowling or sanctimonious so go easy on push pulls. Always use a whisperer to do the dirty work of making the opponents silly, foolish or undependable; you the pristine candidate, should stick to the issues.

Taking Advantage of Whispered Truths

THAT SAID, THE nice thing about a juicy rumor like a DUI is that you can make it even worse by wondering aloud. One whispered story that gives you an idea of the ramifications and why you must be ready with your explanation involves both the former President of the United States, George W. Bush and the former Mayor of Reno. In their past, both GW and the Reno Mayor were reportedly found guilty of a DUI. The story goes in my town that the Mayor, just like President GW Bush, successfully quit drinking. Both men, I suppose are exonerated, recovering, former drunks.

In my first run for city council, I ran against a stellar guy and a wimpy do-nothing guy. I knew that it was going to be easy to beat the second guy because halfway through the primary campaign it was obvious he thought campaigning was limited to getting dressed up and attending parties with his wife.

But the other guy, the stellar one, was going to be tougher. He was a solid and respected former city council person. A whisperer told me about the accusations of corruption in smoke-filled backrooms from the 1950's and 60's—most of the misinformation was perpetuated by the local newspaper (years later the Nevada Supreme court exonerated him) but, even so, the accusations were there.

All I had to do was laboriously check newspaper files, located on reels and reels of microfiche at the local University library, cut and paste up a Unabomber type poster, which I dropped off anonymously at the local newspaper, TV and radio stations; I am not proud of myself.

I won the primary and general election with around 60% of the vote. My happiness was short lived. You won't be safe from the negativity even after the primary or after you win the general and get sworn in. Germaine Greer, a long time feminist, told a group of women, security is when everything is settled, when nothing can happen to you: security is the denial of life. Remember political karma?

Unfortunately, even after the election and the win, people who need to control you will continue to try and break your will. Being secure in preparation, believing in the safety of your memorized community vision values (along with your explanation, justification or apologies), altering your candidate couture to the event, and avoiding body blows from journalists greedy for sensationalism is just the beginning of your political life.

"A black guy was reported running around in his underwear in my front yard when the cops arrived?" I shrieked to a fellow City council member who looked at me a little bewildered. "You knew the mayor was telling that story to people and you didn't tell me?!" (Consider female politicians as both a friend and enemy).

Then I asked the Mayor, "Why didn't you tell me you heard this rumor, instead of perpetuating it?" He wasn't the least bit chagrined; obviously he knew how to play this game, since the sheriff had told him the same underwear story, he had figured it was true. Besides, he told me, "It's in the report." (Consider male politicians as both a friend and enemy).

"Report, I replied, exasperated, "there is no report. It never happened. Stop telling people about this underwear thing, it's a lie."

At the next council meeting, I spotted our tiny, 5'4" former police chief and newly elected county sheriff, surrounded by a group of taller community movers and shakers. I tucked myself into the center of the group, towering over the diminutive lawman. I looked down into his miserable little mustachioed face and asked, "What is this lie you are spreading about an old black guy running around in his underpants in my front yard?" He squirmed and looked me square in the eye and then shirked away.

I found him again, pulled myself in front of him and quietly hissed at him. "Why are you spreading this lie?" Alone, he had no courage. He quickly slid back into his circle of safety. He made a comment. I felt the group turn as if in unison and aim ugly man laughs at my back.

Later that day I phoned the little sheriff and again asked him, why keep the underpants thing alive when he knew it was a lie. He replied, "It's in the report." Somewhat intimidated, very embarrassed and sensibly anguished at the damage he was doing to my reputation, there was nothing else I could do. I just gave up.

Every day in every city and county in this country some sordid underpants character assassination is fabricated from half-truths and innuendo, then repeated over and over.

The 'underwear' style of nasty politics is done for one reason: someone in power thinks you need to be reigned in, and belittling seems to be the avenue men (and some women) often take to attempt the control. In the latest election cycle women were called whores, sluts, prostitutes, ice queens, nutty, extreme, dangerous, wild, and lesbians. They were accused of mistreating undocumented workers, of having a "nice rack" and of attacking the manhood of other candidates. (As when Sharon Angle told Senator Harry Reid, *"Man up Harry."*)

Power on with sincere visions and describe yourself as the inevitable winner of the race. Your job is to convince voters that you care about them—if the voters see you being mean spirited; you may be branded by your own acts.

Nobody listens to a bad person. Remember, political blowback is ugly. It's better to use push pulls along with anonymous telephone surveys, than to look all bitchy, spiteful and smell funny from nervous sweat.

How Many Votes Do You Need to Win?

LET'S CHANGE THE subject from sordid strategies to mathematical algorithms. Do you know how many votes you need to win? There is no such thing as wishing and hoping that you will get enough votes to win. Although I give you an idea of how to find your votes and how many you need to win, don't be slothful; even armed with this secret vote counting information; you still have to work for every single vote.

The odds of winning double or triple if you identify how many votes you need to win and where in your district those voters live. The notion of counting your votes is so simple and so important to the winning ruthless candidate stategy: you are going to scream at us for waiting so long to tell you.

First, Study the Information from the Voter Rolls

THE INFORMATION GLEANED from the voter rolls is invaluable. The cost of the itemized voter rolls is a few pennies a name or even less and it is open information available to anyone. There is no choice, excuse or shortcut about bringing home and examining the voter rolls. Be assured, your opponent(s) are reviewing the rolls too.

The voter rolls tells you how many Democrats, Republicans and Independents are registered in each precinct. It tells you the voters registered names, addresses, date of birth and it even tells if the voter voted in the last four election cycles (primary and general= one election cycle) and what mode they used to vote: by absentee, early voting or in person on Election Day.

The voter rolls will tell you collectively, if the voters in precincts, voted more often for the party or for the person. That information is especially important for down ticket non-partisan candidates. The voter rolls tell you who voted from every precinct but the rolls don't tell you who they voted for. If you look long and hard at the numbers, even that secret is relatively transparent.

Identify the Inveterate Voters

THE LAST FOUR election voting cycles is what I call the inveterate voting cycle. A cycle is a primary and a general. The inveterate code is easily translated campaign lingo, each voter has a string of letters printed just after their name and birth date. The string of letters are a code or an abbreviation that describe the voters recent voting history. Check with your registrar of voters, not every registrar will use the same code.

(V A) (A V) (EV EV) (EV)

V= Poll vote A= absentee EV=early vote blank space = no vote cast.

The voter with a string of all V's and A's will alert the ruthless candidate, that those voters will seldom crossover to vote for a party other than their own, even in non-partisan down-ticket elections. Even more so, if the birth date is before 1960, you can be certain those voters will only vote within their own political party.

The organizational details—using voter rolls, precinct maps and inveterate voter culling—should begin three to four months out from the primary. Reasonably, you will have between 2,000 and 10,000 voters to cull and clarify.

With the historical electorate rolls (aka inveterate voters) it's easy to estimate the number of votes you will need to win your election. First, find the turnout percentage in the most recent similar election.

By similar, I mean compare a presidential election year with a past presidential election or a non-presidential year with a non-presidential year or a special election with a special election. What's important is to not skew the number of votes cast, by comparing apples to oranges. Many more voters come out to vote in a presidential race than in a local non-partisan race, so, never compare votes in a year a President runs for reelection with a year that has only state or local officials running for office.

The rule of thumb for voter turnout:

★ primary-general local election only = low turnout,
★ federal election only = high turnout or
★ primary-general federal election and local elections combined = high turnout.

Costs begin to pile up when you have the voter rolls printed to your specifications. Ask around, you may find the teachers' union or a political party office who will give you the voter rolls piece-meal. Whatever or whoever you must brown nose, do it, because the voter rolls are the key to knocking on the appropriate voter doors.

Calculate the Average Turnout Percentage

TO DETERMINE THE turnout percentage, know the total number of registered voters in each of your precincts. For fear of alienating a voter or depriving a voter of their rights, voter rolls are seldom purged. I can't fix the non-purging problem, but, if you have enough time, purge or cull the rolls yourself.

To cull the voter rolls, call every person listed in the precincts you believe you'll have the most votes. Verify he/she is in fact, the same person(s) living in the residence and is the same person on the roll. It would be nice to know if the voter is still registered in the same political party too.

Often, if the voter has moved, they will be listed twice on the vote rolls, the old residence and the new one too. There is nothing you can do about that—except if the voter is listed twice in your precincts—then of course, you will eliminate the bad address... and hope they don't vote twice. Add to all that drama and confusion, if the telephone number is disconnected, the voter may still live at that address, but no longer use a landline.

Nevertheless, even a cursory attempt at culling the rolls for active voters is better than a blind estimate. However, even armed with culling the rolls, your voter turnout and estimating the number of votes that may be cast for you, will still be a guesstimate. I think it's better to cull the voter rolls than go into a race—blind to the number of vote you need to win.

Another reliable guesstimate is to review the registrar of voters' recap of a previous election similar to yours. Try selecting the last primary election in your district that did (or did not) not have an incumbent running and/or had a similar number of people in the field. Once again, you are looking for a valid number of registered voters who voted in your district on the last Election Day or on the previous comparable Election Day for a down ticket candidate registered in your party. This is the total votes cast. Now you must decide what % you can feasible get.

Another way to find the number of votes needed to win is to use the recap of a similar primary race; list your precinct numbers down the left-hand edge of lined paper. Next to each precinct number, write down the total number of votes of the people *who are designated as a member of your political party affiliation, that voted in a similar election cycle.*

Take the total number of votes from your party affiliation in each precinct and divide that by the total number of votes cast in each of your your precincts; that is the percentage of votes that might be yours, if you were the only candidate running (in your political party). Again, this is another guesstimate that has many variables.

Now you have the probable number of votes both you *and* your opponents (registered in the same political party), may receive. To put a monkey wrench in that vote counting idea: say, you are seeking the county clerk seat and have been seen often with the well-loved and respected incumbent who has decided not to run for another term and he/she is registered in the same political party as you and he/she has publically endorsed you. Then, feasibly you could calculate the number of votes he/she received in the last election and call those votes yours.

To review, if the previous beloved office holder endorses you, and you look talk and act like a professional candidate and you have make a favorable impression when you walked the precinct then probably you will be OK. Granted that idea of vote confidence may be a long shot—you will still have to earn the constituent votes by working hard—but, even so, you could look at those votes another way. Those votes are yours to lose.

District and Precinct Map

DISTRICT AND PRECINCT maps represent a big picture for your campaign strategy, they pinpoint where all of the voters live and give an idea of what your target voters' issues may include. Those precincts are the very ones you cruised through when trying decide what would be your best and most convincing candidate uniform.

If you do not have the district maps with the precincts delineated already pasted on hardboard and resting against a wall in your campaign office, phone the registrar of voters and get them now. There are all sorts of maps issued by your county; be sure to request the most up to date voter precinct maps that include the major arterial roads, schools and landmarks.

The purpose of the district/precinct maps is to plan your walk and talk strategy. When you couple the voter rolls and the precinct maps it will be easy to figure out which precincts could feasibly vote for you and which ones won't give you a second look.

The easiest and simplest way to track your walk and talk progress is to outline precincts with three colored markers: yellow, blue and black. Use a yellow marker to outline precincts where the majority of the voters share your same political party affiliation. The yellow outlined precincts are your base votes. These are the first people you will meet, by walking the precinct and ringing every doorbell, that are affiliated with the same party as yours.

These voters are sacred cows, the voters you can never afford to piss off. They belong to you. Those voters may also be sources of income (cash cows) and voters with whom theoretically you hold a common bond.

Delineate with a blue marker the second best precincts. Second best are the precincts split between Republican or Democrat and Independent voters. Determine your possible votes by checking the voter rolls to find inveterate voters registered in your political party and then add to that number the Independent inveterate voters. If that sum doesn't _outnumber_ the total inveterate voters in the other political party, then it's a tossup if you can win the blue precincts.

This strategy may sound complex; but simply put, if you are a Democrat, precincts that have more inveterate Democrats and Independent voters than Republicans, will often be the precincts you can win. There may be more than one of these multi faceted precincts in your district—trace in blue around the borders of those precincts.

Finally, choose any color you want for the precincts that hold the majority of voters that are in the opposite party (the party you are not registered). Color them whatever marker is available—who cares? Non-party support depends upon your vision statement, how you come across when you debate and speak at their club meetings, how the newspaper places interviews, and finally how you answer their questions; if and when you get around to walking their precincts.

The opposite partisan voters are not yours; they belong to someone else. They probably won't vote for you unless you are kin, belong to the same religion, or if one of their children helped mark their absentee ballot.

Walking the Precincts

I'M NOT SURE why, but people like new politicians to pay their dues.

Voters like the idea that you walked in their precinct. That said, it's imperative to be seen or pretend to be walking precincts in rain, wind and snow.

Voters like to see a clean car parked on a side street with banners plastered on the side. The professionally lettered banner reads simply: "Hi, I'm Michelle Lanphere-Bailey Cando and I am walking your neighborhood right now. I want to talk with you and your neighbors. Vote for Michelle Cando for Water District."

If the precinct is iffy, say predominately registered Republicans: when you are a Democrat, then don't sacrifice mojo, ego or momentum, they probably aren't going to vote outside party lines. Park the car and go have a beer with friends. It is the thought that counts. They will never know if you did or didn't walk the precinct.

When you walk a precinct, you use a walk list. Walk lists are expensive. I always got mine from the teachers union—and they always told me not to tell. Without the walk list, it's a waste of time. Knocking on doors that belong to the opposite party is foolhardy. Who wants to have their feelings hurt or get into an argument with people that would never vote for you anyhow?

Just a reminder, the voter lists reveal who is registered at each house and if they voted in the last election cycle. Usually, you will walk down one side of the street and then down the other side. You should not be knocking on every door—only knock on doors of the voters who are registered in your same political party. When the opposition finds out you are walking the precincts they will get nervous and start walking too.

Door to door techniques vary. Some candidates walk alone, others walk with a child, cute little dog or a volunteer. For safety sake, it is always a good idea to have someone with you. If you walk with a volunteer, he/she stands about five feet behind and carries the walk list on a clipboard. She/he is within listening distance, but not so close as to be obtrusive and part of the discussion.

The volunteer or handler <u>doesn't say anything;</u> she/he just notes any remarks made by the voter, if the voter is positive: a yellow mark is put through his/her name; if negative, a blue or black mark goes through the name. YGA: <u>Y</u>ou have <u>G</u>ot to <u>A</u>sk…. for the vote, even if there is a bad vibe.

You will be way ahead of the game when the voter does most of the talking. It's a good idea to try not to talk about issues that are outside your purview; but then, voters do need a reason to connect. As a council member or school board member, you would have little to do with the Afghan War—but if the voter thinks you feel the same way about the war, he/she is more apt to vote for you.

Do your best not to get into any lengthy explanations about your vision or long conversations about their visions. Keep your statement to the voter simple and to the point. Hello, my name is Randy Pruett, I am running for County commissioner. Please look over these issues and if you think we share many of the same ideas for our town, let me know by voting for me in the primary election.

Often voters will ask you questions. Where do I vote? What is my precinct number? When is the primary? How do I find out if I'm registered to vote? How do I register to vote? Where do I register to vote? You and your handler must know the answers to those questions. Always carry voter registration paperwork and absentee voter applications. Do not fill out the paperwork for the voter.

After two to four minutes when the handler feels you have spent enough time with the voter or the conversation is not going well, the volunteer/handler should step forward and take you gently by the elbow. You will feign surprise and excuse yourself from the voter, "… it was lovely to speak with you. I really hope you will support my campaign. Please call me if there is anything I can do for you."

Hand the voter your business card if you did not get good vibes or give them a walk piece if they seemed to like your message. Consider every person as an opportunity. Just as Judge Bob Coates tells us "meeting people and during the campaign is a gorgeous opportunity to meet hundreds of great people," every person you meet will tell their friends and family about you—they are all important.

If the voter does not answer the door or a child answers the door and you smell dinner cooking—take one of your business cards or walk piece and attach a pre-handwritten post-it note that reads, "I was in your neighborhood and stopped by to hear your ideas about the Parish. Sorry I missed you. Randy"—hand the card to the child and go on your way.

Traditionally, a walk piece is a folded two color shiny professionally printed generic explanation touting your vision speech. Or it's a hit piece, like a contrast/attack comparing you and your opponents visions.

I would like you to go one-step further in the development of the walk piece. It will take more time to develop but it will cost less money. The voter wants and needs a way to connect with the candidate right? An individualized walk piece, tailored to the precinct or neighborhood takes some contemplation and time but that effort will matter heaps to the voter.

Maybe voters want a children's park, graffiti removed, potholes filled or more police protection. Simply take an—in focus—digital snapshot of the controversial or beloved area of the precinct. With either a self inked stamp ordered from a big box store, neatly by hand with a fine tipped black marker or inserted in your campaign font in # 16 campaign font, insert on the upper left hand side one of the following heartfelt statements.

Together we can do great things
Thank you for putting trust in me
I hope we can join as partners to make our neighborhoods a better place.

Here's how you accomplish this personal connection to your voters.

Either use Avery precut postcards or buy a ream of least a #3 weight shiny paper. Deliver to a print shop the photo on a CD or thumb drive. Two hundred cards will equal 50 pieces of #3 or better paper stock. The at home or professionally printed stock must be precisely cut into quarters—most print shops will charge you $1.00 per cut. While you are watching the evening news take a stack of postcards—flip them over and attach a pre-pasted return address label (ordered via the Internet—Creative Labels.com) and sign your name in legible cursive.

Many professional campaign managers believe that door to door canvassing will give you at least 30% of your votes and 50% of neighborhood sign placement. Use your marker pen to color in the precinct as you complete the walk and talks. That way you have a visual of where you have been and where you still need to go.

Plan your weeks and weekends to walk—no matter the weather schedule between 5 and 7 pm. It's your schedule and your decision; but never call or knock on a door after 8:30pm.

Contacting Voters by Phone

A MASS TELEPHONE survey is an excellent way to measure the pulse of the voters. If you are not bucks up enough to hire an interactive touch-tone mass telephone survey or offered an in-kind donation of a telephone bank, you will need to set up your own.

A down ticket telephone bank is a lot like a PTA, teacher or church telephone tree. Each person is given a sheet of voters to take home and phone at their leisure and they will tell you they called them all. Often they are fibbing.

To be sure voters have been called, organize a phone bank. You need about ten people and at least eight phones. Often a real estate office or a union shop has that many phone lines and that many telephones. Nowadays asking eight to ten volunteers to bring their cells phones would work just as well.

Phone bank people and walkers are a shy bunch. They know they want to help—but they aren't prepared for rejection. For that reason, teaching and modeling for the phone bank volunteers is important. Making sure phone bank volunteers are comfortable, well fed and liquored up helps calm their fear of phone rejection. Being prepared means, on phone bank nights the fridge is stocked with beer, wine and caffeinated soft drinks, along with the phone number of a local pizza shop (one that you have previously set up an account). That's how you may get your phone bank people primed.

Give each phone volunteer a voter list and a yellow, blue and black marker plus a sharpened pencil. Each volunteer has a written script: *Hello—I am calling you on behalf of Sandra Cronin, candidate for Mayor. She is asking for your support and vote.*

★ Ring, ring—H*ello* (in a sleepy voice) HANG UP you called a voting sleeper.

★ If the targeted voter hangs up on the volunteer or if the voice mail answers: MAYBE the person will vote for you—put a blue line through the name and send a walk piece and leave a nice short message: " Hello, I hope you will vote for Sam. He thinks the way you do."

★ If the voter says: "I would vote for anyone other than the incumbent. MAYBE the person will vote for you. The candidate must call the next day or that evening. "Anyone" isn't exactly you—so get familiar with this voter.Yellow and Blue line the voter name—that means a better than maybe chance of a vote.

★ YES the voter is yours—Put a yellow line through the name if the voter says they have absentee or early voted for you.

★ NO—Put a black line through the voters name.

★ Can't tell what the voter is thinking—the volunteer then asks the voter, "Oh, the candidate is here—would you like to speak with her?"

Fake it Till You Make It

EVERY TWO WEEKS evaluate where the campaign has been and where it is going. The purpose of this self-assessment and evaluation is to find opportunities to keep the momentum going or to fix the obvious problems.

In order to calculate the likelihood of a win or to be second in the primary, I want you to figure out what information the voters know and/or believe they know about you. Describing the problem is as important as finding a solution. If you deny any responsibility for your waning popularity, the chances of resolving them are small. You may have to do something differently. If you do not change, you will keep getting what you have gotten. Test yourself. What are you willing to do differently in order to win?

What if you have figured out your momentum is waning? Even if you are pissed off and believe your demise is the fault of your opponents or the Chamber or the Carpenters Union don't bemoan your fate. Don't participate in gossip, do not openly criticize the community, your family or anyone—or anything, for that matter. Most of all, never blame journalists for a downward trend. You probably are a long shot anyway—you are having an identity crisis. Reinvent and reevaluate yourself and get down to work.

At least bi-weekly find a quiet comfortable place, free of children, TV and supporters. Analyze if you have followed the ruthless campaign techniques and still do not see or feel a rush of political momentum and inevitability. Ask a trusted person to walk this tightrope with you.

First, make an honest appraisal of your name recognition; is it equal to or higher than the opponents? If not, advertise more, use more signs, show up at more public meetings. The old saw 'absence makes the heart grow fonder' does not apply to a political candidate, so please don't isolate yourself, even if the wind is in your face.

As President Obama said of substance and policy in the 2007 presidential primary race."...this is going to require a new spirit, not of bluster and bombast, but of quiet confidence and sober intelligence, a spirit of care and renewed competence." I want to believe President Obama is talking to you.

Next, examine your issues: is the vision speech and ideology (political party) similar to those of your constituent precinct voters? If it is not too late, change the campaign tone: reevaluate your vision positions and reinforce whatever the precincts/district believes. This is not a flip-flop, rather it's a subtle but impervious change to accommodate base voters. While reassessing the ideology of the district, review the demographics of each precinct. Make sure they are similar to the pedigree you are sporting, if not, improve or dress down the candidate uniform, change voice modulations and again work on the vision speech: maybe it's a little too uppity or not enough.

Finally, review what voters are saying about you. Have you been labeled an outsider, insider, underdog, psycho or flaming liar? If so, change drastically. I would hire a PR firm and knock on every single door in your district in order to prove the whisperers wrong. Sharon Angle, the ballsy Tea Party chick, and an acquaintance, did just that and beat a nice lazy fellow who thought he had a State Assembly seat sewn up tight. Recently, he admitted, *"If I knocked on a door twice, she did it three times."*

You may need to reevaluate where and how you are spending your campaign donations. You do need to spend money to get votes—it's nearly impossible to find every voter at clubs and gatherings. Organize some neighborhood block parties, hold a salad and wine luncheon for your girlfriends, sponsor Cake and Coffee Klatches to discuss local issues and sponsor a team at the annual Komen Race for the Cure.

Review your knowledge about the community issues. Reassess how well you are convincing Titans and voters of your ability to understand and find sensible solutions to local problems. Continue to be an information sponge: understand and ingest every tidbit of information about everyone in the campaign and listen and learn what problems need to be fixed. Always appear confident and appear to be an expert, but never a blowhard.

Reexamine your perceived values. Are you the go-to person and have you demonstrated you are a problem-solver and peacemaker? I trust you have NEVER said, *"That's not my job..."*

While your baggage, aka "the negatives" may be easily defined and a genuine repentance rehearsed, you may have to go deeper into the setbacks and explain with remorse and sincerity. Please do not forget: give an explanation or excuse in five to ten sentences... or less, smile with your eyes and don't droop or shift your shoulders upwards with despair. Then, right away, pivot to the issues the audience is passionate and then talk a lot.

Along with a reevaluation of the campaign, watch and figure out why incumbents are successful. Sometimes, it easy to understand, voters pick the devil they know over the one they don't. Make it public knowledge that you are similar to a beloved incumbent and compare yourself to that revered incumbent.

I hope there has been no ambiguity to what you believe is

intolerable. Announce loudly—abuse to the elderly, women, and children will never be tolerated, and the same goes for driving under the influence, hate crimes, profiling, violation of rights, and cruelty to animals.

Always speak in sound bites when you declare your intolerance. Make some waves and don't be shy—a verbal fight makes news. But remember, voters would rather be happy than angry—use humor when you can.

I strongly believe the voter who denies women an entry-level political job, denies us the right to be leaders both locally and nationally. Because of that strong belief, I beg you not to be a simple woman scared of her shadow; I say, fake it 'til you make it, be a fierce woman running a calculated ruthless well organized campaign.

This speech has been used, however, there is no reason why you cannot accomodate the following speech as your own.

" I would ask for your vote, and your support. I will give it the same energy and determination that I gave everything else in my life, including ...(put your accomplishments here)...so all these things form me and shape me, not just one thing.

It's all the things that I have done in my life, and that's why I believe I can say to you with authority that I am tested, that I am ready and now is the time to vote for me."

TO DO LIST

1. Get a copy of active registered voters who vote in your district
2. Obtain maps of your district with the precincts delineated
3. Make a list of every precinct in your district
4. Cruise the precincts and get to know your district
5. Calculate how many votes you need to win.
6. Pinpoint your base votes on the walk maps
7. Obtain a copy of the incumbent's campaign finance reports from the last election.
8. Get a copy of the financial reports of anyone who has run for the office you are seeking
9. Do some negative research on yourself and make up some excuses.
10. Write a simplified campaign resume or CV
11. Join a Toastmasters Club
12. Get the local newspaper delivered daily to your home
13. Call some old friends and see what they say about you (don't tell them you are running)
14. Call on and review with the Titans of your community what they think are the issues
15. Select your issues and write your vision speech.
16. Write an answer to the question: Why are you running?
17. Find $10,000 for the Primary and $10,000 for the General.
18. Take a black and white headshot and a color family picture & include your parents too.
19. Decide on a campaign font, slogan and color scheme.
20. Order a few lapel nametags and 500 campaign business cards
21. Design a letterhead
22. Use the headshot and campaign resume to design your business card.
23. Put together the Media package: jpeg head shot, resume and vision speech
24. Arrange for a Web site, domain campaign name and Pay Pal.

25. Organize 4-7 campaign uniforms and one or two ensembles to wear with the Titans.
26. File for office
27. Open a bank account
28. Write a begging for money letter
29. Organize a formal expense and revenue reporting system
30. Order a few lawn signs and arterial large signs—buy or solicit rebar and a pounder.
31. Organize a Campaign car kit, Refresher Kit and a tiny "tip and lip" kit
32. Compile a media list
33. Organize a campaign office.
34. Buy stamps, stamped postcards and a self inking stamp with your slogan
35. Order return address labels from an Internet site
36. Write down favors— including dalliances- find a place to hide the good deeds list.
37. Design walk piece for each precinct.
38. Create a three-month calendar— attend 5 events every day.
39. Look for a handler or a driver
40. Manage and organize volunteers for envelope stuffing, walks and telephone trees
41. Organize the precinct maps
42. Organize door to door knock and talks
43. Raise money – ask 5 people for a contribution every day.
44. Evaluate your momentum – reinvent yourself or stay the course.
45. Make news, create controversy, do something newsworthy every week.
46. Project an air of inevitability.
47. Call me, email or check out my blog
48. Thank everyone that does anything for you.
49. Treat every voter like a precious and unique person

About the Author

JUDY DEE HERMAN holds a BA in Business and Sociology from California State University in San Bernardino, as well as certificates in Teaching and Special Education from the University of Nevada, Reno. She's had a long and colorful career—including working for the British Consul and the United Nations in Hong Kong, and IBM in Tokyo, Japan. She served as a councilwoman for the City of Reno and made a run for mayor in 1999. "I have won and I have lost—and winning feels way better." She is currently retired from the Washoe County School District and living in Reno, Nevada.

CPSIA information can be obtained at www.ICGtesting.com
Printed in the USA
BVOW031519070912

299742BV00002B/36/P